ZEROING IN ON NUMBER AND OPERATIONS
Key Ideas and Common Misconceptions, Grades 5–6
Anne Collins and Linda Dacey

P9-DMH-934

Stenhouse Publishers
www.stenhouse.com

Library of Congress Cataloging-in-Publication Data
Collins, Anne, 1950-
  Zeroing in on number and operations : key ideas and common misconceptions, grades 5-6 / Anne Collins and Linda Dacey.
      p. cm.
  ISBN 978-1-57110-798-5 (alk. paper)
  1. Mathematics—Study and teaching (Elementary)—Activity programs.
I. Dacey, Linda Schulman, 1949- II. Title.
  QA135.6.C643 2010
  372.7—dc22
                                        2009050486

Cover design by Designboy Creative Group
Interior design and typesetting by MPS Limited, A Macmillan Company

Manufactured in the United States of America
16 15 14 13 12 11 10   9 8 7 6 5 4 3 2 1

Stenhouse Publishers
Portland, Maine

CONTENTS

Introduction

The development of number sense and computational skills is the most important goal of the elementary and early middle school mathematics curriculum. It takes considerable time and practice to develop these skills and to do so in ways that support understanding, problem solving, and reasoning. "It involves learning powerful mathematical ideas rather than a collection of disconnected procedures for carrying out calculations" (Carpenter, Franke, and Levi 2003, 1). The National Mathematics Advisory Panel (2008) has also identified fluency with whole numbers as essential to later success in algebra, further elevating its importance.

Many teachers feel overwhelmed by the large number of topics they are expected to teach. In response to a curriculum that is criticized for being too wide and lacking depth, the National Council of Teachers of Mathematics (2006) identified focal points for each level from prekindergarten through eighth grade. The National Mathematics Advisory Panel (2008) has also recommended a curriculum that is focused with an emphasis on key topics. At grades five and six, we focus on the key ideas that are essential for success at these levels:

- place value to the billions and the thousandths
- divisibility rules
- division with single-digit and multidigit divisors
- order of operations, including parentheses
- multiples and factors, including least common multiples and greatest common factors
- rational numbers, including equivalence between and among fractions and decimals
- fractions as ratios, including the difference between an additive and a multiplicative relationship
- operations on rational numbers
- ratios and rates

The thirty modules in this flipchart are designed to engage all students in mathematical learning that develops conceptual understanding, addresses common misconceptions, and builds key ideas essential to future learning. The modules are organized in three sections: Whole Numbers and Operations; Fractions; and Decimals. They increase in complexity by section, though we do not assume that you will focus on only one section at a time or that you will necessarily complete each component of every module or section. All modules are appropriate for use with both tier 1 and tier 2 of response to intervention (RTI) as they offer support for students in the regular mathematics classroom and provide suggestions for multiple representations and enrichment as appropriate.

Each module begins with the identification of its **Mathematical Focus** and the **Potential Challenges and Misconceptions** associated with those ideas. **In the Classroom** then suggests instructional strategies and specific activities to implement with your students. **Meeting Individual Needs** offers ideas for adjusting the activities to reach a broader range of learners. Each activity is supported by a reproducible (located in the appendix), and **References/Further Reading** provides resources for enriching your knowledge of the topic and gathering more ideas.

We encourage you to keep this chart on your desk or next to your plan book so that you will have these ideas at your fingertips throughout the year.

REFERENCES/FURTHER READING

Carpenter, Thomas, Megan Franke, and Linda Levi. 2003. *Thinking Mathematically: Integrating Arithmetic and Algebra in Elementary School*. Portsmouth, NH: Heinemann.

National Council of Teachers of Mathematics (NCTM). 2006. *Curriculum Focal Points for Prekindergarten Through Grade 8 Mathematics: A Quest for Coherence*. Reston, VA: NCTM.

National Mathematics Advisory Panel. 2008. *Foundations for Success: The Final Report of the National Mathematics Advisory Panel*. Washington, DC: U.S. Department of Education.

Millions and Billions

Mathematical Focus

- Extend place-value knowledge to millions and billions.
- Develop a sense of the magnitude of very large numbers.
- Associate real-world situations with very large numbers.

Potential Challenges and Misconceptions

Young children are given frequent opportunities to associate numbers with real collections of objects, and as they get a bit older, they see models of a hundred and a thousand as well. These associations allow students to develop a sense of the size of these numbers. Unfortunately, students do not always develop models for how big the numbers a million and a billion really are.

Our classroom practices can also foster misconceptions. We usually use word names to communicate these large numbers, and the word *billion* looks a lot like the word *million*, making it easy for some students to conclude that the size of the numbers must also be similar. When students see 1,000,000 and 1,000,000,000, they are quite surprised by how different these numbers look and are more likely to recognize that there are 1,000 millions in a billion. Further, we often refer to millions, billions, and trillions, much as we mention ones, tens, and hundreds in the earlier grades. Except for when we are looking at a place-value chart, we rarely talk about ten millions or hundred millions in the classroom. The result is that many students (and adults) think of billions as one place to the left of millions, making them 10 times, rather than 1,000 times, as great.

In the Classroom

There are many ways to engage students in thinking about these large numbers. You might choose a question such as the following:

- Would you rather have a thousand dollars or a million pennies?

- How old is someone who has lived for a million seconds? A billion seconds?
- How many blades of grass do you think there are in a baseball field?
- How much space would it take to hold a million one-dollar bills?

It is important to capture students' initial intuitions right away. The range in responses is likely to be great. We frequently ask groups of teachers to estimate the equivalent of a million seconds and receive answers ranging from one hour to a century. (They're actually equivalent to about 11.5 days.) Seeing the wide range helps everyone appreciate how much we don't know. Following this initial reaction, allow students to talk in small groups, use calculators to carry out some computations, or conduct experiments, whichever is best for the question you have posed. After discussing their results, have students explore the questions in the *Thinking About Millions and Billions* reproducible on page A1 of the appendix.

Students will enjoy sharing their responses. Be sure to provide time for students to identify how they arrived at their answers and space in the classroom to display their answers and techniques.

Meeting Individual Needs

You can give some students only the top portion of the *Thinking About Millions and Billions* reproducible, focused exclusively on millions.

For students who are ready, suggest that they explore the same questions about a trillion.

REFERENCE/FURTHER READING

Ellett, Kim. 2005. "Making a Million Meaningful." *Mathematics Teaching in the Middle School* 10 (8): 416–23.

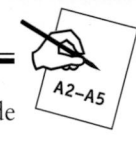

Mathematical Focus

- Deepen understanding of the numerical value of digits in large numbers.
- Apply understanding of place value to problem situations.

Potential Challenges and Misconceptions

Achieving mastery in understanding place value is an ongoing process. Students in grades five and six need to engage with interesting mathematical activities designed to deepen and apply their understanding of place value. Noted physicist Richard Feynman once wrote, "I learned very early the difference between knowing the name of something and knowing something" (Feynman and Leighton 2001, 13–14). The greatest challenge facing teachers is helping students develop facility with and knowing the importance of place value rather than just memorizing the names of the places in which the digits reside.

In the Classroom

Make at least three copies of both the direction cards and digit cards from the *Place-Value Game Cards* reproducible on pages A2–A4 of the appendix. Decide if you want pairs of students to work with millions, billions, or trillions. (You may need more copies of the digit cards when working with trillions.) Give each pair a set of direction cards and a set of digit cards. Tell the students how many digit cards should be turned faceup between them (seven for millions, ten for billions, and thirteen for trillions).

Following are the directions for playing the *Place-Value Game* in pairs:

1. Players take turns. On each turn, take one direction card from the pile and place it faceup between you.
2. After turning over the direction card, each player should use the digits to make a number that best matches the direction card.

3. Each player records the number he or she has made in his or her notebook.
4. Players compare numbers to see which one best fits the direction card. The student whose number best matches the direction card earns 1 point. The player with the most points at the end of the game wins.
5. Continue playing until you have turned over all the direction cards.

As students play the game, it is informative to listen to them discussing their strategies or justifications for why they think they made the greatest or least number, sum, difference, or product. Listening to student conversations often uncovers misconceptions of which you were not aware. For example, one student was overheard saying, "The value of the 3 in the number 673,492,108 is two times bigger than the value of the 9 because it is two places to the left."

Meeting Individual Needs

Decide how much support you will offer individual students based on their past experiences with place value. Students who have not had a wealth of experience with place value may benefit from a number line model. Students who have demonstrated an understanding of place value, but who make computational errors, may benefit from additional activities that blend place value and computational practice. A sample of such an activity is *What Is the Mystery Number?* (see the reproducible on page A5).

REFERENCES/FURTHER READING

Feynman, Richard, and Ralph Leighton. 2001. *What Do You Care What Other People Think? Further Adventures of a Curious Character.* London: Norton.

Van de Walle, John, Karen Karp, and Jennifer Bay-Williams. 2010. *Elementary and Middle School Mathematics: Teaching Developmentally.* 7th ed. New York: Pearson Education.

Fact Practice

Mathematical Focus
- Practice basic facts.

Potential Challenges and Misconceptions

There is a difference between practice and drill. Practice means we are doing mathematics that we have recently learned in an attempt to achieve proficiency. Drill is activity designed to promote automaticity and speed in recall. Timed tests or quizzes are considered drill and often cause more anxiety in students who do not work well under pressure. We all need practice in mathematics, activities designed to engage us in working without the pressure of being timed. It is essential to include regular, interesting, practice activities in mathematics to ensure students recognize that mathematics is a discipline in which they can excel with enough practice and that the practice can be fun.

In the Classroom

There are multiple engaging ways to help students practice various computations.

- *T Challenge:* All students participate in this activity. As many students as possible work at the board and each begins by drawing a very large *T.* Students who do not fit at the board participate by using either individual boards or recording sheets with a number of large *T*s already on them. The teacher dictates random numbers, which the students record on the left side of the large *T.*

  The teacher then identifies the operation, which students record above the list of dictated numbers, and the addend, subtrahend, or factor, which students record above the right-hand column. For example, the teacher may say, "Times six." All students record the $\times$ 6 and begin computing. (See figure.)

$$
\begin{array}{c|c}
\times & 6 \\
\hline
7 & \\
2 & \\
9 & \\
4 & \\
11 & \\
8 & \\
\end{array}
$$

Once the students are finished, they put down their chalk or markers and turn around or, if the students are at their seats, hold up their small boards or recording sheets. Either a student or the teacher reads out the correct answers.

Students keep the original list of values for the next challenge but erase their *answers.* The teacher chooses a student to name the next operation and addend, subtrahend, or factor for the next challenge. The challenges may include only basic facts. For example, the student might say, "Plus eight," "Minus seven," or "Times nine."

This activity can be adapted to include division. When students are ready, challenges may include directions such as "Add twenty-five," "Multiply by one hundred," "Subtract one-fourth," and "Divide by negative two."

- *Math Wonder:* Students use the *Math Wonder* reproducible on page A6 of the appendix to practice computation. This is a self-correcting activity since it is designed so that the starting number recurs in each starburst if the student calculates accurately.

Meeting Individual Needs

The *T Challenge* activity is designed to allow the teacher to see at a glance which students have mastered a particular times table or have the ability to add or subtract as well as those who need more practice or a specific intervention.

You can tailor the *Math Wonder* activity for individual students by carefully selecting the starting value for them.

REFERENCE/FURTHER READING

Ebdon, Susan, Mary Coakley, and Danielle Legnard. 2003. "Mathematical Mind Journeys: Awakening Minds to Computational Fluency." *Mathematics Teaching in the Middle School.* NCTM: 9 (8): 486–93.

Mathematical Focus

- Use prime factors to develop divisibility rules.
- Multiply or divide.

Potential Challenges and Misconceptions

By definition, a prime number is a positive integer that has two and only two unique positive factors. One example of a prime number is twenty-nine, which has only two positive factors: one and twenty-nine. The two most pervasive misconceptions that students demonstrate when discussing prime and composite numbers are that one is a prime number and that all prime numbers are odd. It is important to be very explicit that one is a special number, as it has only one unique factor, and that two is the only even prime number.

In the Classroom

The *Sieve of Eratosthenes* is an algorithm designed to identify prime numbers. Give students a copy of the *Sieve of Eratosthenes* reproducible on page A7 of the appendix and instruct them to put an *X* through the 1. Conversation about the number one is appropriate at this time and should include the fact that it is a special number that is neither prime nor composite. Next, have students circle the 2, draw a line through all the multiples of two, and write the factor 2 under each of those multiples. Students continue by circling the 3, drawing a line through all multiples of three, and listing the factor 3 under each multiple. If the number already has a line through it, students still draw another line through it and record the new factor alongside any other factors. For instance, the 6 will have two lines through it and the factors 2 and 3 below it. (See figure.)

A copy of the completed Sieve of Eratosthenes is located in the Answer Key at the end of the book.

Throughout this activity, remind students to make a list of any patterns they notice. Following are some questions you might ask:

- What do you notice about the unmarked numbers? (They are prime numbers.)
- What do you notice about the numbers that have two lines through them? (They are composite numbers and have at least two prime factors in addition to one and themselves.)
- What do you observe about the digits in numbers that are divisible by three? (The sum of the digits in a multiple of three is also a multiple of three.)
- What conjecture can you make about numbers that are divisible by six? (They are also divisible by both two and three.)

Meeting Individual Needs

Students who rely on a visual representation of various patterns can use different colors to fill out the Sieve of Eratosthenes. One caution with using colors is that many students are color-blind.

For students who would enjoy a challenge, ask them to determine why they can stop circling primes at 7.

REFERENCE/FURTHER READING

Quesada, Antonio. 1997. "Recent Improvements to the Sieve of Eratosthenes." *Mathematics Teaching in the Middle School* 90 (4): 304–7.

Prime Builders

Mathematical Focus
- Identify and find the prime factorization of any positive integer.
- Apply divisibility rules.

Potential Challenges and Misconceptions

When we represent the prime factorization for a number, we are actually identifying the longest string of factors a number has. The prime factorization of a number is unique; that is, there is one and only one set of prime factors for any given number. Too often we have students determine prime factorizations through rote techniques. Such procedures are often forgotten and students don't develop full appreciation for this concept, which is so important to applications of number theory.

In the Classroom

Use different shapes and assign a prime number to each shape. (See figure.)

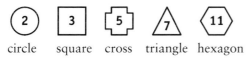

circle   square   cross   triangle   hexagon

Display these shapes and assigned values in a prominent location. Place a large number of the shapes in a sack so they are not visible to students. Select two to six of the shapes and announce their product to the class or a small group. Challenge the students to determine how many shapes you selected and what value they have.

One sixth-grade teacher introduces this activity as a guessing game. Each time a student calculates the correct factors and shapes, he instructs the student to share the strategy he or she used to find the prime factors. After a student shares a strategy, the teacher asks if anyone did it differently or if anyone got a different answer. Through this sharing, he can identify any misconceptions the students have. After a few examples, he gives students the opportunity to discuss some strategies for determining the chosen shapes. He then explains that what they are discovering is *the prime factorization of a number* and gives them an opportunity to try to figure out what shapes would be needed to show the prime factorization for 105.

Over time, his students practice two strategies for finding the prime factors when given a product. (Sample practice problems are included in the *Building Prime Factorization* reproducible on page A8 of the appendix.) If, for example, the product is 105, they can use a tree diagram or repeated division:

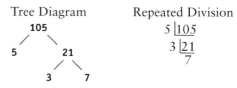

The prime factorization is $5 \times 3 \times 7$. (one square, one cross, one triangle)

When he discusses the repeated division method, he asks his students to think individually about how they can determine with which divisor they should start. After providing no more than a minute for the students to think individually, he asks the students to discuss their strategies in small groups and allows them two minutes for this sharing. After the sharing time, each group reports out its strategies, which he records on a conjecture board before discussing the divisibility rules. If any of the conjectures do not always work, he erases them from the conjecture board. (Note: A conjecture board is similar to a parking lot. It is a place where students' observations, hypotheses, and ideas are recorded until they can be disproven either by a counterexample or by negation. Using a conjecture board is an informal method for introducing the concept of proof.)

Meeting Individual Needs

If you are sure none of your students is color-blind, you can substitute colored tiles or colored candies (if you are able to use candy in the classroom) instead of shapes to represent the prime factors.

For students who struggle with computation, you can allow the use of a times table chart or a calculator. The use of these aids will not interfere with the reasoning that must precede use of these tools.

REFERENCE/FURTHER READING

Davis, Brent. 2008. "Is 1 a Prime Number? Developing Teacher Knowledge Through Concept Study Preview." *Mathematics Teaching in the Middle School* (14) 2: 86–91.

Mathematical Focus

- Link the operation of multiplication to the operation of division.
- Use a multiplication menu to divide.

Potential Challenges and Misconceptions

Division is performed either to determine how many groups can be made (measurement or quotative) or to determine an amount of something that will be shared fairly or equally among a given number of groups (partitive). Since many students view division as an operation separate from multiplication, it is helpful, even advisable, to explicitly connect the two operations.

It is also important to recognize that for many students the long-division algorithm causes difficulties.

A multiplication menu incorporates friendly factors and operations; that is, numbers and computations that most students find accessible (e.g., multiplying by ten, doubling products, halving products, and adding factors and their products).

Suppose you are trying to determine how to distribute 480 fairly among 32 groups. A problem may read: *Jimmy has 480 marbles. He has 32 marble bags. If he puts the same number of marbles in each bag, how many marbles will each bag hold?*

Set up a multiplication menu as follows:

1. Begin by listing the multiplicative identity: 32×1.
2. Next multiply by 10 (an easy fact): 32×10.
3. Halve the previous product to find 32×5.
4. Add the products of 32×10 and 32×5 for the product of 32×15.

Multiplication Menu	
32×1	$= 32$
32×10	$= 320$
32×5	$= 160$
32×15	$= 480$

Therefore, Jimmy would place fifteen marbles in each of the thirty-two bags.

In the Classroom

One of the most important considerations when discussing partitive division is to think about and refer to the dividend as a quantity that is being distributed. This means that if you are dividing 480 objects into 32 groups, the conversation should stay focused on those quantities as you build the multiplication menu. Beginning with the multiplicative identity and using friendly numbers help students develop their number sense. The divisor, in this case 32, is used to build the multiplication menu. As the students become more adept at building the menu, they often demonstrate an uncanny ability to hone in on a closer estimate of the quotient than when they are first introduced to this procedure.

As students become comfortable with using multiplication menus, you can increase the size of the numbers. For example, you can introduce this problem: *Mario wants to share his baseball card collection of 4,235 cards with his class of 35 children. How many cards will each student receive?*

Examine the multiplication menu for $4,235 \div 35$ in the figure.

Multiplication Menu		
35×1	$= 35$	
35×10	$= 350$	(multiply 1×35 by 10)
35×20	$= 700$	(double 10×35)
35×100	$= 3,500$	(multiply 10×35 by 10)
$3,500 + 700 + 35 = 4,235$		
$35 \times (100 + 20 + 1) = 35 \times 121 = 4,235$		

Based on the multiplication menu, students should determine that Mario will give each student 121 baseball cards.

Meeting Individual Needs

Few students actually begin using the multiplication menu as efficiently as it was designed, and that is okay. Some students may need to make up to ten entries in their menus before they capture a close quotient. Still other students may apply a particular quotient that results in the necessity to do repeated computations.

With time and experience, most students will become efficient with this method and very adept at estimating quotients. Practice problems are provided in the appendix reproducible *Multiplication Menus and Division* on page A9.

REFERENCE/FURTHER READING

Van Putten, Cornelis, Petra van den Brom-Snijders, and Meindert Beishuizen. 2005. "Progressive Mathematization of Long Division: Strategies in Dutch Primary Schools." *Mathematics Teaching in the Middle School* 36 (1): 44–73.

Understanding Division Algorithms

Mathematical Focus
- Model traditional division algorithms.
- Explain the steps within traditional division algorithms.
- Make connections among various constructed algorithms, the traditional algorithm, and a variety of recording schemes.

Potential Challenges and Misconceptions

Among our traditional algorithms, division is often the least understood. This algorithm differs from the others in a variety of ways, including that it works left to right, rather than right to left; it also involves multiplication, subtraction, and estimation; and when you transpose a division problem to the algorithmic format, you need to change the order of the numbers: $72 \div 9$ becomes $9\overline{)72}$.

We sometimes teach division in ways that further exaggerate these difficulties. Students may only be told to follow the four-step cycle of *d*ivide, *m*ultiply, *s*ubtract, and *b*ring down, and to memorize meaningless phrases such as *dirty monkeys smell bad* to trigger the correct order of steps, without any conceptual development. In the earlier grades we emphasize the fair-sharing or partitive model of division, as children are familiar with sharing objects among friends and wondering how many each friend will get. Conversely, the language associated with the traditional algorithm emphasizes the measurement model of division, with phrases such as *how many fours are there in seventy-two?* (Gregg and Underwood Gregg 2007). To make matters worse, students often hear phrases such as *six goes into seventy-two*, and sometimes *goes into* is pronounced as *gozinta*, ensuring all meaning is lost.

In the Classroom

A fifth-grade teacher is working with a small group of students. These students have constructed division techniques with which they are comfortable, many of which rely on multiplication. A few of these students have learned the traditional algorithm, while others have never seen it. Today the teacher wants this group to think about the traditional algorithm and be able to explain it to others. He poses the following problem and asks students to solve it. Note that he purposely poses a relatively simple problem with a sharing context.

> The department secretary has 563 stamps to give to 4 workers. She has 5 sheets of 100 stamps, 6 strips of 10 stamps, and 3 single stamps. How many stamps should each worker get?

A couple of students share their techniques and then the teacher calls on a student who has used the traditional algorithm. Though the student can clearly follow the steps, she cannot explain why she is doing so. The teacher says, "Let's model this problem and then compare what we do with what was just written." He places paper plates and base ten blocks on the table for the students to use.

Two of the students spread four plates across the table and another says, "We should give everybody a hundred right away." They place a hundred block on each plate, leaving representations of one sheet of one hundred, six strips of ten, and three single stamps to distribute.

The teacher then says, "Before we do any more, I want you to look at the written work and show me where we represented what we just did."

With the teacher's help the students continue to work back and forth between the model and the traditional algorithm. They also make connections among the other recordings and the traditional recording and decide the secretary should keep the three remaining stamps.

Later in the week, the group explores examples with two-digit divisors and the students complete the task in the *Show How It Works* reproducible on page A10 of the appendix. Then they compare their techniques in pairs. If neither used the traditional technique, they try it together.

Meeting Individual Needs

The *Show How It Works* reproducible on page A10 of the appendix allows you to enter numbers appropriate for each student.

Students in other countries, such as Brazil, learn to record division differently. Should you have students with different backgrounds, be sure to include their representations in discussions.

REFERENCES/FURTHER READING

Gregg, Jeff, and Diana Underwood Gregg. 2007. "Interpreting the Standard Algorithm in a 'Candy Factory' Context." *Teaching Children Mathematics* 14 (1): 25–31.

Martin, John F. Jr. 2009. "The Goal of Long Division." *Teaching Children Mathematics* 16 (8): 282–87.

Greatest Common Factors and Least Common Multiples

Mathematical Focus
- Find the greatest common factor.
- Identify the common multiples.
- Use a Venn diagram to organize data.

Potential Challenges and Misconceptions

Students who engage in rote learning without conceptual understanding often develop serious misconceptions. When finding the least common multiple for nine and fifteen, one student listed the product and its equivalent prime factors shown on the left. Then he crossed out two 3s, as shown on the right.

$$9 = 3 \times 3 \qquad 9 = \cancel{3} \times 3$$
$$15 = 3 \times 5 \qquad 15 = \cancel{3} \times 5$$

His teacher asked why he crossed out the 3s and he replied, "Because they are the same." The teacher then asked if he could cross out the other 3 since it, too, was the same. He replied, "Sure, you can cross out as many as you want." He went back to his notation and crossed out the third 3 and declared the least common multiple was five. He knew a procedure but did not understand the underlying concepts.

In the Classroom

Tape two large embroidery hoops on the board using duct tape. Next to the two wooden hoops, tape a second set of two overlapping embroidery hoops. Place a large array of sticky notes with prime factors on them on the board near the hoops. Be sure to have multiple copies of the prime numbers 2, 3, 5, and 7. (See figure.)

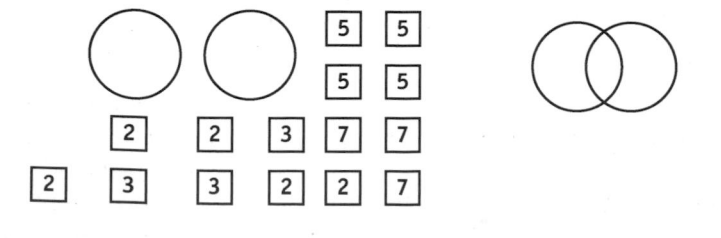

Provide students with a *Venn Diagram* recording sheet (see page A11 in the appendix) and small sticky dots on which they can write prime factors. Begin by asking students to find the prime factors

of sixteen and twenty-four. Demonstrate by placing the sticky note factors in the first set of hoops. (See Figure 1.)

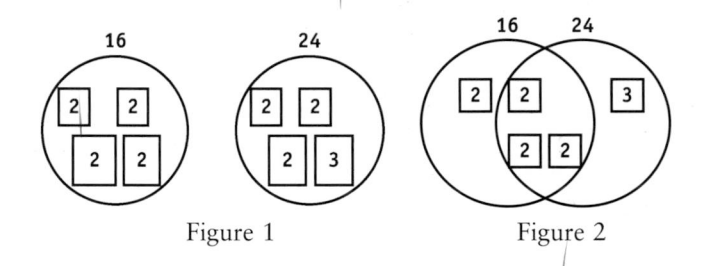

Figure 1   Figure 2

Ask the students to discuss in small groups how they might represent the overlap of factors. Record student responses on a conjecture board. Demonstrate the pairing of the common factors, and place the pairs in the intersection of the second set of two hoops. (See Figure 2.)

> ### Conjecture Board
> *Shared factors only get shown once.*
> *Shared factors go in the middle of the two hoops.*
> *The product of the factors in the middle of the two hoops is 8.*
> *Factors that aren't shared stay in the big circles.*
> *Shared factors are common factors, so the common factors are $2 \times 2 \times 2$.*

Instruct the class to discuss, in small groups, whether any of them can be used to help find the *greatest common factor*. Students usually agree that $2 \times 2 \times 2$, or 8, is the greatest common factor (GCF). Challenge the students to decide if and how they can use the Venn diagram to determine the *least common multiple* (LCM).

Meeting Individual Needs

The amount of time individual students need using the sticky notes, hoops, or Venn diagrams varies. Students should be allowed to use them as long as they deem necessary. Students who need a challenge may be asked to make conjectures about additional ways for finding greatest common factors and least common multiples.

REFERENCE/FURTHER READING

Bradley, Elizabeth. 1999. "Finding Common Ground." *Teaching Middle School Mathematics* 5 (4): 236.

Problem Solving with Greatest Common Factors and Least Common Multiples

Mathematical Focus

- Solve problems that apply the greatest common factor and least common multiple.
- Use a graphic organizer to develop and support mathematical vocabulary.

Potential Challenges and Misconceptions

There is widespread confusion among fifth- and sixth-grade students around the concepts of factors and multiples. One effective way to avoid this confusion is to consistently use the vocabulary of factors and multiples each and every time students work on multiplication and division. The numbers being multiplied are the factors; the product is the multiple. When there is no remainder in division, the divisor is also a factor of the dividend, with the quotient being the second factor. Using the terms *product* and *multiple* interchangeably and using *factor*, *multiplier*, and *multiplicand* interchangeably are effective ways to help students differentiate between factors and multiples.

Asking students to solve interesting and relevant problems using greatest common factors (GCFs) and least common multiples (LCMs) is also an important way in which to ensure students are correctly differentiating between the two. Sample problems are provided in the *For What Am I Looking?* reproducible on page A12 of the appendix.

In the Classroom

One way to address misconceptions with the terms *factor* and *multiple* is to have students develop their own glossaries. Following is a sample graphic organizer (see *Vocabulary Builder* on page A13 of the appendix for a reproducible version). Students build the meaning of a word in stages.

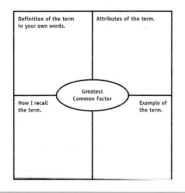

Some teachers substitute *Nonexamples of the term* for the *Attributes of the term* region, since they find some students benefit from identifying what is and what is not an example. Most students begin by completing the *Example of the term* region.

From there they either fill in the *How I recall the term* region or the *Attributes of the term* region.

The last region that students tend to complete is the *Definition of the term in your own words* region. Once they do, you should ensure their definition is mathematically correct.

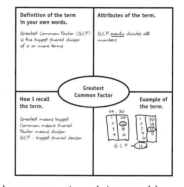

Students need to engage in solving problems similar to those included in the *For What Am I Looking?* reproducible if they are to internalize the conceptual difference between GCFs and LCMs. Such problems also help students gain a better understanding of the usefulness of these concepts in real-world situations.

Meeting Individual Needs

Ask students who are struggling to break the problem solving into two parts. First, ask the students to read through the problems and identify if they are seeking the LCM or the GCF. Once they have correctly identified the appropriate concept, they can proceed to solve the problems.

REFERENCE/FURTHER READING

Cai, Jinfa. 2003. "What Research Tells Us About Teaching Mathematics Through Problem Solving." In *Teaching Mathematics Through Problem Solving: Prekindergarten–Grade 6*, ed. Frank Lester Jr. and Randall I. Charles, 241–53. Reston, VA: National Council of Teachers of Mathematics.

Working with Remainders

Mathematical Focus

- Solve division problems.
- Interpret remainders.

Potential Challenges and Misconceptions

Research provides evidence that students do not know how to interpret remainders in division problems. Part of the challenge is due to the fact that most of the division problems students are assigned have "naked" numbers—that is, computation without a context. Many students just report the answers to division problems as 24 R2 or 8 R3 (Van de Walle, Karp, and Bay-Williams 2010). With a context students might note, "I have twenty-four groups and two more toward a twenty-fifth group," or "Each person in the group gets eight objects and I discarded the extra three because it is not fair for some to get nine and others eight."

In the Classroom

One teacher illustrates the concept of sharing a fractional component of the original set of objects by passing out forty-two packages of stickers to her eighteen students. When all the students receive two packets, the teacher breaks down the remaining six packets and distributes additional individual stickers to each student. Each student receives two full packets and one-third of a packet. The teacher also repeats this activity using play money. She distributes $5.00 in play money to each student and asks the class what she should do with the $9.00 she has left. The students unanimously agree that if she converts the $9.00 into quarters, each will receive two quarters, or an additional $0.50.

To illustrate the appropriateness of discarding the remainder when dividing, one teacher passes out thirty-seven homework passes to the twenty-five students in her class. Each student receives one homework pass, but twelve students get an additional pass. The thirteen students who receive only one pass complain vigorously.

Some students say, "That's not fair."

Others state, "Everyone should get the same number of passes."

The teacher explains, "After I passed out the first twenty-five, I still had thirteen left over, so I passed them out as well."

She then asks her students what they would have done. The overwhelming response is "Save the extra passes until you have enough for everyone to get a second pass."

On another day, she uses a field trip the class is planning to discuss remainders. She engages the class in helping her decide how many buses the fifth and sixth grades would need if each bus held 42 people and there were 181 students and chaperones. The students work in small groups to determine that it would take four full buses. They agree that the 13 people who would not fit in the four buses would require them to order a fifth bus.

Students who must reason through various situations that involve division and remainders are more likely to understand the connotations of remainders than students who learn procedures in isolation. Sample problems with contexts are provided in the *Making Sense of Remainders* reproducible on page A14 of the appendix.

Meeting Individual Needs

Students who struggle to understand what to do with remainders often benefit from writing their own division problems. To best engage these students in reasoning about remainders, ask them to write four distinct problems that have a remainder of two. In one problem it should make sense to round down the quotient, in a second problem it should make sense to round up the quotient, in a third problem it should make sense to write the remainder as a decimal, as in money problems, and the fourth problem should require the remainder to be used as a fraction, such as $3\frac{1}{2}$ cookies.

REFERENCES/FURTHER READING

National Research Council. 2001. *Adding It Up: Helping Children Learn Mathematics.* Washington, DC: National Academy Press.

Schwartz, James. 2008. *Elementary Mathematics Pedagogical Content Knowledge: Powerful Ideas for Teachers.* Boston: Pearson.

Van de Walle, John, Karen Karp, and Jennifer Bay-Williams. 2010. *Elementary and Middle School Mathematics: Teaching Developmentally.* 7th ed. New York: Pearson Education.

Estimating Quotients

Mathematical Focus

- Extend estimation skills to include estimating quotients.
- Check estimation of quotients using a calculator.
- Estimate answers to problems that do not need an exact answer.

Potential Challenges and Misconceptions

Many students mistakenly believe that estimation means you complete the computation and then round the answer up or down. Estimation requires students to consider the magnitude of the dividend in relation to either the number of groups (divisor) that can be made or the amount of objects that can be evenly shared among a specified number (divisor) of people. Close estimations of quotients require a deep understanding of the relationship between multiplication and division.

Rounding often plays a prominent role in the estimation of sums, differences, and products. For example, to estimate 39×52, we might round each factor to the nearest ten and find $40 \times 50 = 2,000$. However, it is no easier to estimate $4,000 \div 70$ than $4,321 \div 73$. Some students might consider $4,000 \div 100$, but to estimate more closely, it is usually best to round the dividend to the nearest multiple, so in this case, it would be better to consider $4,200 \div 70$. Note that this skill relies heavily on the ability to recall and use basic fact knowledge.

In the Classroom

Students benefit from immersion in estimation activities. Estimation should be embedded in the process of learning and understanding all mathematics. One obvious way in which to engage students in making sense of estimation is to ask students to predict the quotient before computing the answer. A second part of the prediction process necessitates contextual problems, activities, and tasks. Following are some activities that are appropriate for building estimation sense.

- Pair students. Provide each pair with a list of division problems. Prompt students to identify the number of digits that will be in the quotient. For example:

- Pair students. Provide each pair with a list of division problems. Prompt students to identify the computation that will result in the greater quotient. For example:

Identify the greater quotient.

Explain how you know. Check your answers using a calculator.

- Play *Estimation Bingo*. Make copies of the 4-by-4 Bingo board in the *Estimation Bingo* reproducible found on page A15 in the appendix. Pair students. The first student to fill in four squares either horizontally, vertically, or diagonally wins the game.

- Have students solve problems that require estimation. For example:
  The sixth-grade class at Memorial Middle School has raised $13,579 toward its trip to Washington, DC. If it costs between $150 and $175 per student to attend, about how many students can go on the trip?

Meeting Individual Needs

Building estimation skills is a process. Students who struggle to estimate quotients or determine what to do with remainders benefit from more estimation exposure. You can modify each of the activities described previously with smaller dividends until students demonstrate the number sense needed for estimation.

To further challenge students, create an *Estimation Bingo* sheet on which you fill in appropriate values in Part A and estimated quotients on the game board, and ask the students what values could appear in Part B.

REFERENCES/FURTHER READING

Lampert, Magdalene. 1992. "Teaching and Learning Long Division for Understanding in School." In *Analysis of Arithmetic for Mathematics Teaching*, ed. Gaea Leinhardt, Ralph Putnam, and Rosemary A. Hattrup, 221–81. Hillsdale, NJ: Erlbaum.

Star, Jon, and Bethany Rittle-Johnson. 2009. "It Pays to Compare: An Experimental Study on Computational Estimation." *Journal of Experimental Child Psychology* 102 (4): 408–26.

Mathematical Focus

- Simplify expressions.
- Compute using the order of operations.

Potential Challenges and Misconceptions

Understanding the conventions of mathematics is not always easy for students, but it is important for them to realize that since mathematics is the language of the universe, it would cause mass confusion if everyone did mathematics differently. Understanding the *order of operations* convention is a fundamental skill for students learning mathematics. Many young students have been told to do all their computation from left to right when expressions are written horizontally. It is so important that as teachers we do not make absolute statements that do not hold true in all circumstances. Use of the mnemonic device *please excuse my dear aunt Sally* and other such sayings actually promote misconception. Students recite the saying but neglect to include that we multiply or divide from left to right or add or subtract from left to right. As a result they may think they should multiply before they divide when finding $320 \div 4 \times 20$, which will give the answer 4, instead of the correct answer, 1,600.

In the Classroom

Since the order of operations is a fundamental concept that applies throughout the study of mathematics, it is important that students learn and understand this convention. There are many different ways to engage students in simplifying expressions.

- *Round-Robin with Order of Operations*: Group students in threes. Assign each student in each group a number: one, two, or three. Call out any number to start, for example, the number two. Each student assigned number two goes to the board. This student records the expression you call out. For example, the expression might be $50 - 2(7 + 2 \times 6) - 5$. The student at the board completes the first step in simplifying the expression by writing $50 - 2(7 + 12) - 5$. Then this student sits down and the student assigned number three goes to the board and completes the next step: $50 - 2(19) - 5$. Then the student assigned number one goes to the board and completes the next step: $50 - 38 - 5$. The students continue to rotate in this fashion, recording $12 - 5$ and finally, 7.

  Playing this round-robin game allows students to work collaboratively and help each other if there are incorrect computations, and it allows the teacher to informally assess students' understanding of the order of operations.

- *Where Do the Operators Go?* The goal for this activity is to create an expression to get the largest value possible. Students work in pairs. They use a deck of playing cards from which the face cards have been removed. Each student receives a set of cards from the *Order of Operations Cards* reproducible on page A16 of the appendix. The students deal out six cards. Both students use the six cards and their operator cards to make the greatest value possible. Students must keep the cards in the order they were turned over, positioning them from left to right, they *may not* combine digits to make two or three digit numbers. They may use as few or as many operator cards as they wish. The student who makes the greater value takes all the cards. If both students make the same value, each keeps his/her own cards. For example, if the six cards are 573921, one expression might be $5(7 + 3 \times 9)^2 - 1$, which simplifies to 5,779. A second expression may be $5 \times 7 + 3^9 + 2 \div 1$, which simplifies to 19,720. Play continues until the students can no longer deal out six cards at once. The player who has collected the most cards wins.

- *Four Fours*: Students complete the *Four Fours* reproducible on page A17 of the appendix. They begin working individually but if they get stuck, they may collaborate with a partner. They may use any of the four operations, parentheses, raise a four to the power of four, the factorial symbol ! (which represents $4 \times 3 \times 2 \times 1$), and the square root symbol to make as many of the number sentences true as possible.

Meeting Individual Needs

All students must become proficient at working with multiple operations within one expression, equation, or problem. Many students stumble because of their lack of automatization of the basic addition or multiplication facts. Since the focus of these activities is on the order of operations, it is appropriate to allow students to use an addition or multiplication table. We do not suggest they use any calculator that builds in the order of operations, since that would defeat the purpose of the activities. But students could use a calculator with the order of operations built into it to check their computation.

REFERENCES/FURTHER READING

Campbell, Stephen, and Rita Zakis, eds. 2002. *Learning and Teaching Number Theory: Research in Cognition and Instruction*. Westport, CT: Ablex.

Gawronski, Jane, Marthe Craig, Mary Eich, and Kim Morris. 2005. *Mathematics Assessment Sampler, Grades 3–5: Items Aligned with NCTM's Principles and Standards for School Mathematics*. Reston, VA: National Council of Teachers of Mathematics.

National Mathematics Advisory Panel. 2008. *Foundations for Success: The Final Report of the National Mathematics Advisory Panel*. Washington, DC: U.S. Department of Education.

Adding and Subtracting Fractions with Pattern Blocks

Mathematical Focus

- Model addition and subtraction of fractions.
- Add halves, thirds, and sixths.
- Subtract halves, thirds, and sixths.

Potential Challenges and Misconceptions

"No one knows better than teachers who have had experience teaching fractions that current instruction is not serving many students" (Lamon 1999, 4). One of the reasons that learning about fractions can be challenging is that whole number ideas dominate students' thinking. When adding fractions, students commonly add both the numerators and the denominators and conclude, for instance, that $\frac{2}{3} + \frac{5}{6} = \frac{7}{9}$. Students need a firm grasp of the meanings of the numerator and denominator as well as to understand conceptual models of addition and subtraction.

Students often draw pictures to represent their thinking when working with fractions. The difficulty with using circles, rectangles, and even student-drawn number lines is that the parts are most often not equivalent and may reinforce misconceptions. The use of student-drawn circles to represent fractions is especially problematic since students do not measure the central angles. In fact, when a circle has eight regions, we say each represents one-eighth without ensuring each central angle is actually 45 degrees. Estimates like these contribute to misunderstanding in geometry and measurement. After you have documented student understanding that fractional regions must be congruent, it is acceptable for students to use a sketch of a circular whole if they use it only to count up the number of parts compared with the whole.

In the Classroom

If your students have not modeled fractions with pattern blocks, have them find ways to build the hexagon using only blocks of one color. Then ask what the values of the triangle, the larger rhombus, and the trapezoid would be if the hexagon were one whole. If you do not have pattern blocks available to you, make three copies of the *Pattern Blocks* reproducible on page A20 of the appendix and have students cut out the pieces. If you have access to the Internet, you can find pattern block shapes at the National Library of Virtual Manipulatives (go to http://nlvm.usu.edu/en/nav/vLibrary.html).

One teacher begins by reminding students that we add and subtract like things; that is, we might find that seven robins and five robins make twelve robins. If we were to add seven robins and five sparrows, we would need to find a noun to describe both groups, for example, *birds*. He then gives a counterexample: If a team scored four touchdowns and three field goals, we can't say that it scored seven touchdown field goals.

Using the relevant pattern block pieces, he tells the students to take a rhombus and a triangle and put them together. He asks students to identify the addition sentence this represents if the hexagon is one whole. Once students agree it is $\frac{1}{3} + \frac{1}{6}$, he says, "Now to add, we have to have the same things. How can we find a common name for what we have?"

Jason suggests *two pieces*, and everybody agrees that would work, but Mario points out that they probably need to find a fraction.

Lupé says, "Three triangles can cover these blocks, so it could be three-sixths."

Emma then suggests that the pieces make a trapezoid, so the answer could be one-half. (See figure.)

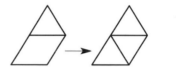

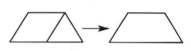

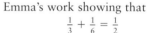

Lupé's work showing that $\frac{1}{3} + \frac{1}{6} = \frac{3}{6}$ Emma's work showing that $\frac{1}{3} + \frac{1}{6} = \frac{1}{2}$

Students explore three more addition sentences: $\frac{1}{2} + \frac{1}{3}$; $\frac{2}{3} + \frac{5}{6}$; and $1\frac{1}{2} + \frac{1}{6}$. Next the teacher asks students how they could model $\frac{2}{3} - \frac{1}{6}$. They decide to get two rhombi, cover up a triangle, and name what is left. Once he is sure students understand the pattern block model for addition and subtraction, he gives them copies of the *Pattern Blocks* reproducible on page A20 of the appendix and challenges them to complete the problems on the *Modeling Addition and Subtraction with Pattern Blocks* reproducible on page A21 of the appendix. He reminds his students that the hexagon represents the unit.

Meeting Individual Needs

Some students will need many examples of adding fractions using the pattern blocks while other students will need only a few examples. For students who catch on immediately, tape two hexagons together and define this shape as one whole, allowing students to explore examples with fourths and twelfths as well.

REFERENCES/FURTHER READING

Lamon, Susan. 1999. *Teaching Fractions and Ratios for Understanding.* Mahwah, NJ: Erlbaum.

Phillip, Randolph, and Cheryl Vincent. 2003. "Reflecting on Learning Fractions Without Understanding." *On-Math* 2 (2): 1–6.

Mathematical Focus

- Add and subtract fractions.
- Add and subtract mixed numbers.

Potential Challenges and Misconceptions

Too often teachers rush to teach or tell students how to do procedures rather than let the students explore contextual situations that require computation. The informal methods students use to compute with pattern blocks, fraction strips, or Cuisenaire rods set a foundation that allows students to see what a sum or difference might be. Van de Walle, Karp, and Bay-Williams (2010) stress the need for students to use invented strategies when working with fractions since they illustrate a student's number sense.

In the Classroom

Students respond favorably to solving problems that lead to computational procedures. Consider posing a series of scaffolded questions that lead to the concept of common denominators. One teacher asks her students to show her two different ways to solve the following problem:

> Sasha shoveled $\frac{1}{4}$ of the driveway and Lily shoveled $\frac{5}{8}$ of it. How much of the driveway was shoveled?

After solving the problem, two students share their thinking with the class.

- Jill: I made a picture to show how much Sasha shoveled. Then I made another picture the same size to show how much Lily shoveled. I had to cut the picture in half to show eighths.

When I did that, I thought it would make sense to cut Sasha's into eighths so I could just count up all the eighths.

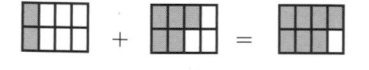

When I wrote it out, it looked like this.

$$\frac{1}{4} + \frac{5}{8} = \frac{2}{8} + \frac{5}{8} = \frac{7}{8}$$

- Max: I thought that $\frac{5}{8}$ is the same as $\frac{1}{2}$ plus $\frac{1}{8}$. I also thought that $\frac{1}{2}$ is the same as $\frac{2}{4}$, so I added $\frac{1}{4}$ plus $\frac{2}{4}$, which equals $\frac{3}{4}$. So I know they shoveled $\frac{3}{4}$ plus $\frac{1}{8}$. I also know that $\frac{3}{4}$ equals $\frac{6}{8}$ and $\frac{6}{8}$ plus $\frac{1}{8}$ is $\frac{7}{8}$.

The teacher challenges the students to come up with an algorithm for adding fractions. She lists their conjectures on the conjecture board. (See figure.)

> ### Conjecture Board
>
> - *Make the denominators the same, then add the numerators.*
> - *Find equivalent fractions that have the same denominator, then add.*
> - *Find a denominator all the fractions share, then add the numerators.*

The class discusses each conjecture. It revises the second conjecture until all the students agree that to add fractions, you must have a common denominator. If you don't, it is important to find equivalent fractions that have the same denominator, which stays the same while you add the numerators.

Next the teacher poses a problem that includes mixed numbers. Again, she asks the students to solve it in two different ways.

> Bill had $3\frac{1}{4}$ pounds of jelly beans. He ate $\frac{7}{8}$ pounds before giving the rest to his mother. How many pounds did he give to his mother?

After giving them time to work, she asks two students to explain how they solved the problem.

- Carly: I drew pictures that I made into eighths. I counted the number of eighths I had, then subtracted $\frac{7}{8}$. I started with $\frac{26}{8}$ and took away $\frac{7}{8}$. I had $\frac{19}{8}$ left over. I changed that back to $2\frac{3}{8}$. So, $\frac{26}{8}$ minus $\frac{7}{8}$ equals $2\frac{3}{8}$.

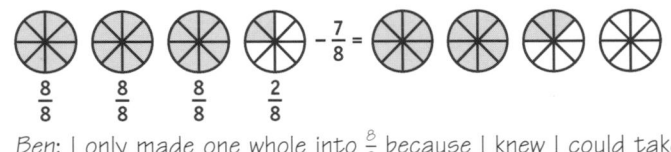

- Ben: I only made one whole into $\frac{8}{8}$ because I knew I could take $\frac{7}{8}$ from it. So I wrote:

$$2\frac{2}{8} + \left(\frac{8}{8} - \frac{7}{8}\right) \qquad 2\frac{2}{8} + \frac{1}{8} = 2\frac{3}{8}$$

To end the class, the teacher challenges them to complete the *Problems with Fractions* reproducible on page A22 of the appendix.

Meeting Individual Needs

Some students will insist it is important to have the least common denominator, but that is not important at this stage. Encourage students to use manipulatives as long as they need to. Many students will benefit from practicing with fractions without a context to solidify proficiency with the processes.

REFERENCE/FURTHER READING

Van de Walle, John, Karen Karp, and Jennifer Bay-Williams. 2010. *Elementary and Middle School Mathematics: Teaching Developmentally.* 7th ed. New York: Pearson Education.

Modeling Multiplication of Fractions

Mathematical Focus

- Model multiplication of fractions with pattern blocks.

Potential Challenges and Misconceptions

Without models and representations that make sense to students, they often are confounded when multiplication of fractions yields a product that is less than either or both factors. The standard algorithm for multiplication of fractions is fairly simple and often masks lack of understanding of the concept. Students need time to develop their number sense with fractions and to adjust the thinking that results from their familiarity with multiplying whole numbers. The repeated addition model of multiplication offers a simple beginning and then students can move to the array or area model.

In the Classroom

One teacher introduces multiplication of fractions using pattern blocks. Her students are familiar with the blocks and can readily identify that if the hexagon is one, then the trapezoid is one-half, the larger rhombus is one-third, and the triangle is one-sixth. She begins by posing a problem and asking students pairs to model it with the blocks.

> Ms. Chow is making puppets. She needs $\frac{1}{2}$ of a yard of brown felt to make one puppet. How many yards of brown felt does she need to make 6 puppets?

The students model the $\frac{1}{2}$ yard of cloth with the trapezoid and then gather six trapezoids, one for each puppet. Next the students reconfigure the trapezoids to form three hexagons and identify the total amount of cloth needed as 3 yards. The teacher records the multiplication sentence on the board, that is, $6 \times \frac{1}{2} = 3$ and asks students to record sketches of the pattern block model and the associated number sentence in their notebooks. Next they do the same for the expressions $4 \times \frac{1}{6}$ and $4 \times \frac{2}{3}$.

The teacher purposely began with whole number multipliers so that students could gain confidence and understanding, but now she thinks they are ready for more of a challenge. She poses this problem:

> Mr. Mendes is making cookies. The recipe calls for 2 cups of flour for each batch. He wants to make $2\frac{1}{2}$ batches of cookies. How much flour does he need?

The teacher asks, "How is this problem like the one about the puppets?" Mason replies, "You need so much to make one and then you need that amount several times." The students are again asked to model the problem with the blocks, find the answer, and record their work in their journals. Some pairs aren't sure what to do after identifying four hexagons as the way to show what is needed for two batches. Then Emily explains, "If he's making half of a batch, he'll need half as much flour, or one cup."

Once everyone agrees that $2\frac{1}{2} \times 2 = 5$ and that Mr. Mendes needs 5 cups of flour, the teacher queries, what if each batch called for $2\frac{1}{3}$ cups of flour? Through discussion the students agree that the problem can be modeled by using the blocks shown in the figure and that $2\frac{1}{2} \times 2\frac{1}{3} = 5\frac{5}{6}$. Note that as with whole numbers, the distributive property of multiplication over addition allows us to think of $2\frac{1}{2} \times 2\frac{1}{3}$ as $2 \times 2\frac{1}{3} + \frac{1}{2} \times 2\frac{1}{3}$.

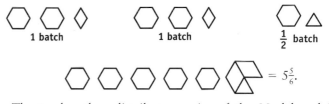

The teacher then distributes copies of the *Model and Solve* reproducible on page A23 of the appendix for students to complete.

Meeting Individual Needs

As modeling multiplication is the goal, all students should have pattern blocks available for use. If you do not have these materials make several copies of the *Pattern Blocks* reproducible on page A20 of the appendix and have students cut out the pieces. Note that some students may prefer to merely draw representations, without first using the blocks, and this is fine. For students ready for more challenge, have them write word problems for the expression $3\frac{2}{3} \times \frac{1}{2}$.

REFERENCE/FURTHER READING

Geist, Eugene. 2009. *Children Are Born Mathematicians*. Old Tappan, NJ: Pearson Education.

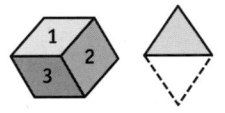

Mathematical Focus

- Model division of fractions with pattern blocks.

Potential Challenges and Misconceptions

How many adults were taught this rule for dividing fractions: Yours is not to reason why; just invert and multiply? Few adults and fewer students can explain why inverting and multiplying works. Most are also surprised when an expression such as $2 \div \frac{1}{3}$ results in a quotient of 6, which is greater than either the dividend or the quotient. As one student asks, "How did we get more than we started with?"

It makes more sense, therefore, to ask students to demonstrate concretely what happens in division of fractions. The measurement model of division, which focuses on finding the number of groups when the size of the groups is known, is the easiest model to represent and so that is the best place to begin. Once again we suggest the use of pattern blocks, which can be particularly effective in helping students understand why division with fractions may result in a quotient greater than the divisor.

In the Classroom

Say you have $\frac{1}{2}$ cup of molasses, and a loaf of anadama bread requires $\frac{1}{6}$ cup of molasses. How many loaves can you make? The question posed can be simplified to *How many one-sixths are there in one-half?* With our pattern block model, the task becomes that of determining the number of triangles, which have a value of $\frac{1}{6}$, that is equal to the trapezoid, which has a value of $\frac{1}{2}$. Some students build with triangles either on top of or beside the trapezoid to form the same shape. Others tend to "stamp" the trapezoid with the triangle to find how many there are. As it takes three triangles to cover the trapezoid, we know that one-half divided by one-sixth equals three. (See figure.) There are three sixths in one-half.

Provide students a variety of examples to model with the blocks and encourage them to record sketches of the representations, along with the associated number sentences, in their notebooks or journals. Begin with expressions that result in whole number quotients. For example, $3 \div \frac{1}{6}$, $2\frac{2}{3} \div \frac{1}{3}$, and $4\frac{1}{2} \div \frac{1}{6}$. Students tend to become confident in this task rather quickly. To help encourage efficiency over time, ask questions such as, *How could we determine the number of sixths in three wholes without counting each one?*

When students are ready, present an example that results in a quotient with a fraction. Though they may not experience difficulty modeling the problem, students are likely to be challenged to

name the answer. For instance, to model $1\frac{1}{6} \div \frac{1}{3}$, a hexagon and triangle are used to model the dividend and the task is to determine the equivalent number of thirds or rhombi. As shown in the figure, there are three thirds in the whole, but only half of a whole in the sixth. Thus $1\frac{1}{6} \div \frac{1}{3} = 3\frac{1}{2}$.

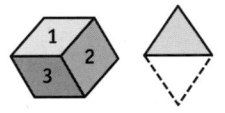

A common misconception would be to identify the quotient as $3\frac{1}{6}$. Students' attention must be directed to the idea that the one-sixth must be compared to the one-third, the unit we are counting. With practice, students will grasp this idea, but many examples and teacher modeling may be needed. Because this concept challenges adults as well, another example is provided.

To find $2\frac{1}{3} \div \frac{1}{2}$, model $2\frac{1}{3}$ with two hexagons and one rhombus and determine the equivalent number of trapezoids (halves).

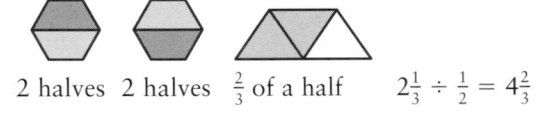

2 halves   2 halves $\frac{2}{3}$ of a half $2\frac{1}{3} \div \frac{1}{2} = 4\frac{2}{3}$

To provide further attention to the conceptual meaning of division with fractions, have students complete the tasks on the *Understanding Division with Fractions* reproducible on page A24 of the appendix.

Meeting Individual Needs

As with multiplication of fractions, the standard division algorithm is simple, but the conceptual underpinnings are complex. Some students may need to model the process for a significant amount of time, particularly when the division results in a fraction. It may help some students to write *I am counting <u>thirds</u>*, for example, when solving $2\frac{1}{2} \div \frac{1}{3}$.

REFERENCE/FURTHER READING

Neuman, Dagmar. 1999. "Early Learning and Awareness of Division: A Phenomenographic Approach." *Educational Studies in Mathematics* 40 (2): 101–28.

Multiplying Fractions with Arrays

Mathematical Focus
- Multiply fractions using an array model.

Potential Challenges and Misconceptions
Too many students do not understand that anytime any two numbers are multiplied, they make a rectangle. Think about a common explanation for why we multiply. Many students are told that multiplication is a fast way of adding. That may be so at times, but more often this idea interferes with students' thinking about multiplication on a deeper level. When we find the product of two-thirds times one-fourth, we are not using multiplication as a quicker way to add.

In the Classroom
Use an array model for multiplication to set a stage for recognizing that multiplication involves two dimensions, a length and a width. When we are multiplying fractions by fractions, the array model is a rather powerful representation of why and when a product can be less than either of the factors being multiplied. One teacher brings in some crispy marshmallow treats she has made in an $8\frac{1}{2}$-by-11-inch baking pan so that the students' models can exactly replicate the whole. She gives each student several pieces of paper from the recycling bin and poses the following problem.

> If I gave $\frac{1}{2}$ pan of these treats to Emilio, how much would he get?

She lists on the overhead $\frac{1}{2}$ of 1 pan. She asks the students to fold one sheet of the paper to model what is happening while she actually cuts the pan of treats and then removes one-half of the treats from the pan. She records on the board $\frac{1}{2}$ of 1 pan $= \frac{1}{2}$ pan, and the students fold their papers vertically, shade in one side to show one-half of one pan, and record the statement $\frac{1}{2}$ of $1 = \frac{1}{2}$ in their notebooks. (See figure.)

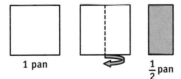

1 pan $\frac{1}{2}$ pan

The teacher then asks the students to think about how much of the original amount of treats a student would receive if she were given one-half of the remaining half of the pan of treats. She models what would happen with the actual treats, cutting the remaining half pan into one-half. She records her activity directly underneath her previous sentence.

$$\frac{1}{2} \text{ of } 1 \text{ pan} = \frac{1}{2} \text{ pan}$$
$$\frac{1}{2} \text{ pan of } \frac{1}{2} \text{ pan} =$$

Before she fills in the result, she asks her students to fold their papers (the same ones with which they started) in half horizontally. Then she instructs them to shade the part that represents the one-half

of one-half. After they open their papers, she asks them what part of the whole they have left. After the students respond, she has them compare their results with what she has left in the pan of treats before they complete the chart.

$$\frac{1}{2} \text{ of } 1 \text{ pan} = \frac{1}{2} \text{ pan}$$
$$\frac{1}{2} \text{ of } \frac{1}{2} \text{ pan} = \frac{1}{4} \text{ pan}$$

Next students explore two-thirds of two-thirds. The teacher begins by writing directions for finding the product on the conjecture board. (See figure.)

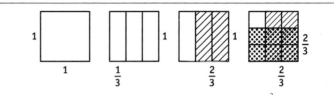

- *Fold the paper into thirds vertically. Shade in $\frac{2}{3}$.*
- *Fold the paper into thirds horizontally. Shade in $\frac{2}{3}$ using a different color or pattern.*
- *Count the total number of squares for the denominator. Count the number of squares shaded in by both colors or patterns for the numerator.*

The students determine that the product is four-ninths.

Most students benefit from recording the factors and products in an organized table.

To support the students' move to a pictorial stage, the teacher asks them to make sketches in their notebooks of what they have done.

Lastly, the teachers asks the students to solve the problems on the *What's My Product?* reproducible on page A25 of the appendix.

Meeting Individual Needs
An effective way to help students develop an understanding of multiplication of fractions is to provide them with multiple experiences that move from the concrete to the pictorial to the abstract. The paper folding is the concrete stage of development. The length of time students need to fold paper varies. To reinforce the process of folding paper, ask students to sketch the process in their notebooks. It is from the table, the drawing, and your guiding questions that students are able to see patterns that lead them to identify an efficient way to multiply fractions.

REFERENCES/FURTHER READING
Coulson, Tim. 2006. *Maths Misconceptions*. National Numeracy Strategy. Teacher Magazine 42. www.teachernet.gov.uk/teachers/issue42/primary/features/Mathsmisconceptions/.

Lamon, Susan. 1999. *Teaching Fractions and Ratios for Understanding*. Mahwah, NJ: Erlbaum. 93–109.

McCormack, Steve. 2006. "Maths Misconceptions." *Primary Teachers Magazine* (January).

Dividing Fractions with Area Model

Mathematical Focus

- Divide fractions.
- Divide fractions using an area model.

Potential Challenges and Misconceptions

Many students are confused about division of fractions. Often they mistake dividing by one-half with taking one-half, or dividing by two. They may also be confused with the idea that in division of fractions, the result may be larger than the values they are dividing. Liping Ma (1999) documented the struggle people have when asked to write a story problem for the computation $1\frac{1}{2} \div \frac{3}{4}$. She found that most could not identify an appropriate context for the computation.

In the Classroom

One teacher begins each class with a formative assessment of students' prior knowledge. Before beginning any discussion about division of fractions, she poses a *range question* to her students. Range questions are short examples or quick computations that allow a teacher to gauge the range of understanding among the students in her class. Often she discovers the students have a deeper understanding of a concept than she originally assumed. She might instruct them, "Turn to your partners and tell them three things you can about $1\frac{1}{2}$ divided by $\frac{3}{4}$." Or she might request, "Write a story problem for $\frac{2}{3}$ divided by $\frac{1}{4}$." The results of the student responses inform what she does next.

During her lessons, she poses "families" of examples and calls upon her students to report their results and strategies. Following are some sample problems:

1. *I have 2 pounds of gummy bears that I am going to share equally with my friend. How much will each of us receive? How do you know?*
2. *I have 1 pound of gummy bears that I am going to share equally with my friend. How much will each of us receive? How do you know?*
3. *I have $\frac{1}{2}$ pound of gummy bears that I am going to share equally with my friend. How much will each of us receive? How do you know?*
4. *I have $\frac{1}{4}$ pound of gummy bears that I am going to share equally with my friend. How much will each of us receive? How do you know?*

After working on this set of problems, the students report their findings. Comments include:

- Each time the gummy bears are shared, the amount each person gets is smaller.
- We noticed that when the number of pounds was half of the time before, the amount each person got was also half the amount of the time before. Like $\frac{1}{2}$ divided by 2 equals $\frac{1}{4}$; then $\frac{1}{4}$ divided by 2 equals $\frac{1}{8}$.
- We got a common denominator and divided. So for $\frac{1}{2}$ divided by 2, we said $\frac{1}{2}$ divided by $\frac{4}{2}$ equals $\frac{1}{4}$.

The teacher then moves on to problems that include contexts that are best represented by drawing squares. If, for instance, you are trying to determine how many *individual* two-thirds servings can be cut from three-quarters of a pan of brownies, it makes sense to draw a square pan. The serving size requires eight of the twelve rectangles formed by the intersection of the brownies and the serving size. (See figures.)

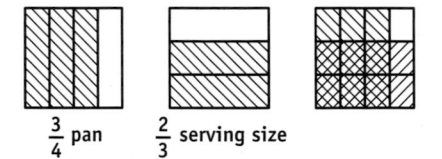

$\frac{3}{4}$ pan $\frac{2}{3}$ serving size

If we reposition the rectangles to cover only the area that contains brownies, we can see that there is 1 complete serving size plus 1 of the 8 we need to make the next serving size. So, $\frac{3}{4} \div \frac{2}{3} = 1\frac{1}{8}$ servings. (See figure.)

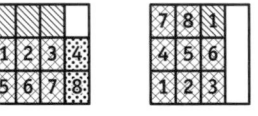

After doing two or three examples, she assigns problems for the students to represent and solve, such as those in the *Let's Share or Group!* reproducible on page A26 of the appendix.

Meeting Individual Needs

Regardless of the representation students use, it is helpful to provide templates for students so the fractional pieces are equivalent. Templates for division with fractions are provided in the *Area Division of Fractions* reproducible on page A27 of the appendix.

Some students struggle with the area model and benefit from numbering the pieces they need to make a serving. (See figure on left.)

When it is time to determine the solution, it helps to number all the rectangles from 1 to 8. Each set of eight is one serving size, and the remaining piece is a portion of the next eight pieces needed for the serving size. (See figure on right.)

This represents $1\frac{1}{8}$ servings from $\frac{3}{4}$ pan of brownies when the serving size is $\frac{2}{3}$.

REFERENCES/FURTHER READING

Ma, Liping. 1999. *Knowing and Teaching Elementary Mathematics.* Mahwah, NJ: Erlbaum.

Van de Walle, John, Karen Karp, and Jennifer Bay-Williams. 2010. *Elementary and Middle School Mathematics: Teaching Developmentally.* 7th ed. New York: Pearson Education.

Posting Problems with Fractions

Mathematical Focus
- Pose problems that involve fractions.
- Add, subtract, multiply, and divide fractions to solve problems.

Potential Challenges and Misconceptions

In classrooms, word problems generally provide the question to be answered, along with the exact information required to find that answer. As you know, it doesn't work that way in the real world, where we generally have to formulate the questions ourselves and then find the data necessary to answer them. To be better prepared for applying their mathematical skills to the real world, students need opportunities to pose problems, not just to solve them. Posing problems builds on curiosity while strengthening students' understanding of mathematics and their familiarity with the language of mathematics. In fact, David Whitin suggests, "problem posing is an adventure waiting to happen" (2006, 18).

It is particularly important for students to have opportunities to pose problems related to fractions. Too often, both adults and students are unable to pose even simple word problems for number sentences with fractions. Thinking about questions to ask requires students to focus on the meaning of the four basic operations, something that can be forgotten when whole numbers are no longer the focus.

In the Classroom

Teachers should model problem-posing behavior, to make questions that begin with *What if* or *I wonder what* common within their classrooms. One teacher shares with her class that she read in the newspaper that five-sevenths of the last seven elected presidents have been left-handed. She tells the students that it made her wonder about the fraction of the students in their school who are left-handed. On another day, she tells them that she recently read about a fish that was only about one-third of an inch long and added that she wondered how many of those fish it would take to make a line as long as the largest fish ever caught. Such questions might lead to mathematical investigations or prompt students to share number-related questions they have wondered about, too. Through her behavior, the teacher is suggesting that there are lots of interesting math-related questions to ask and to answer.

You can use problem starters, such as newspaper articles, pictures, equations, graphs, or problems without questions, to help students pose their own problems. One teacher presents students with the following information and asks them to think of questions they could answer using the given information:

> Today Emma ran around the $\frac{1}{4}$-mile track 18 times. Will ran $\frac{1}{2}$ of the total distance that Emma ran. Will ran $\frac{3}{4}$ of a mile longer than Dan did. Dan wasn't feeling too well today. He loves running and usually goes around the track 21 more times than he did today.

Students brainstorm several questions, including the following:

- *How many miles did Emma run today?*
- *How many times did Will go around the track?*
- *How many miles does Dan usually run?*
- *How many more miles did Emma run than Will did today?*

Then the teacher asks students to choose three of the questions on the list and answer them.

The *Posing Problems* reproducible on page A28 of the appendix provides some problem starters. Here are some other ways to help students pose problems:

- Remove the questions from traditional textbook problems.
- Present students with a bar graph for which they must pose fraction-related questions.
- Provide students with words and numbers, for example *woods*, *picnic*, and *hike* and $\frac{1}{8}$, $2\frac{1}{4}$, $\frac{3}{4}$. Have students write math problems using all of the words and all of the numbers.
- Give students a page from a supermarket flyer and have them pose and answer three math problems using the given information.
- Have students brainstorm mathematical questions they can ask about their favorite card games, board games, or sports.
- Have each student interview a parent or caregiver about the types of arithmetic problems he or she solves. Then the student can write a problem about one of the situations identified.
- Identify a portion of a bulletin board where students can post interesting math-related questions that begin with *I wonder*.

Meeting Individual Needs

Students often pose problems appropriate for them to solve. Similarly, they usually choose problems at their level to solve. Working in pairs can help students who are less sure how to begin or who are less confident with open-ended tasks. In relation to the track example, a student might pose a problem such as *How many miles did Will run?* Another student might pose a problem that suggests more complex thinking, like *What fraction of Dan's usual distance did Will run today?* Encourage students to share their problems so that they can consider other types of problems.

REFERENCES/FURTHER READING

Barlow, Angela, and Jill Mizell Drake. 2008. "Assessing Understanding Through Problem Writing: Division by a Fraction." *Mathematics Teaching in the Middle School* 13 (6): 326–32.

Baxter, Juliet. 2005. "Some Reflections on Problem Posing: A Conversation with Marion Walter." *Teaching Children Mathematics* 7 (3): 122–28.

Whitin, David. 2006. "Problem Posing in the Elementary Classroom." *Teaching Children Mathematics* (13) 1: 14–18.

Mathematical Focus

- Solve addition, subtraction, multiplication, and division problems using equivalent fractions.

Potential Challenges and Misconceptions

Combine problem solving and fractions, and you have identified the greatest challenge upper elementary and middle school teachers and students face. In fact, most teachers suggest their students convert all fractions to decimals before computing. This advice serves as a flag to students that fractions are hard and are to be avoided at all costs. This is far from the truth. With support and appropriate materials, all students can and will develop the confidence they need to work comfortably with fractions.

In the Classroom

The best way to become a good problem solver is to solve problems. Similarly, the best way to become proficient with fractions is to work with fractions. In one classroom, students spend most of their time working with problem-solving situations, but they also engage in class activities that build proficiency in computation involving fractions. Their teacher uses the *Math Wonder* and the *T Challenge* activities (see "Fact Practice") to assess students' proficiency with computation.

Students work in groups of three to solve problems. Each student is given a number: one, two, or three. Each number is assigned a role; for example, one day students with the number one are the recorders, students with the number two are the reporters, and students with the number three are the managers. The recorder ensures the group has a consensus representation of its work; the reporter goes to the overhead or document camera and shares the group's work; and the manager ensures the group answers the question, has the materials it needs, and stays on task. The responsibilities rotate daily.

One day the teacher assigns this problem:

Katie made four cups of lemonade. Emmet drank a third of that lemonade. How many cups of lemonade were left?

Jeff shares his group's strategy.

We drew four measuring cups.

Each measuring cup was filled. He drank $\frac{1}{3}$, which left $\frac{2}{3}$ cups in each measuring cup for a total of $\frac{8}{3}$ or $2\frac{2}{3}$ cups.

On another day, the teacher assigns a problem that combines least common multiples with fractions as the unit of time.

Rowen, Gunner, and Conor run $\frac{1}{3}$, $\frac{1}{5}$, and $\frac{1}{6}$ of a lap per minute, respectively. How many laps do they need to run to cross the finish line at the same time?

Students work in groups to solve this problem. One group draws an oval to represent the track. The students use red to mark thirds, blue to mark fifths, and black to mark sixths all the way around the track. They list how long each person takes to complete a lap in an organized table under the oval.

$\frac{1}{3}$	3	6	9	12	15	18	21	24	27	(30)
$\frac{1}{5}$	5	10	15	20	25	(30)	35	40		
$\frac{1}{6}$	6	12	18	24	(30)	36				

They explain that Rowen ran ten laps, Gunner ran six laps, and Conor had to run only five laps.

A second group reports it noticed that if the fractions were whole numbers, the least common multiple for three, five, and six would be thirty. The students determined that if they found equivalent fractions all of which had thirty as the denominator, they would know how many laps each runner would have taken when the three runners were at the same spot. They show their equivalent fractions as $\frac{1}{3} = \frac{10}{30}$; $\frac{1}{5} = \frac{6}{30}$; and $\frac{1}{6} = \frac{5}{30}$. They conclude by stating the numerators are the number of laps and the denominator is when all the runners were together.

This teacher saves the most efficient strategy for the last class report so students with various strategies are able to share their work first.

Meeting Individual Needs

One way to challenge students and yet support those students still in need of scaffolding is to offer problems that differ in difficulty. In the *Problem Solving, Part One* and *Problem Solving, Part Two* reproducibles on pages A29 and A30 of the appendix you will find problems at two levels. The problems on the first reproducible are appropriate for all students, while those on the second one are more challenging. The more practice students have with solving problems with fractions and listening to multiple strategies, the more likely they are to become adept at solving them.

REFERENCES/FURTHER READING

Kamii, Constance, and Mary Ann Warrington. 1999. "Teaching Fractions: Fostering Children's Own Reasoning." In *Developing Mathematical Reasoning in Grades K–12, 1999 Yearbook of the National Council of Teachers of Mathematics,* ed. Lee V. Stiff and Frances R. Curcio, 82–91. Reston, VA: National Council of Teachers of Mathematics.

Van de Walle, John. 2003. "Designing and Selecting Problem-Based Tasks." In *Teaching Mathematics Through Problem Solving: Prekindergarten–Grade 6,* ed. Frank Lester Jr. and Randall I. Charles, 67–80. Reston, VA: National Council of Teachers of Mathematics.

Making Sense with Thousandths

Mathematical Focus

- Extend place-value knowledge to thousandths.
- Develop a sense of the size of thousandths.
- Identify numbers represented by a variety of collections of ones, tenths, hundredths, and thousandths.

Potential Challenges and Misconceptions

When teachers first introduce tenths and hundredths, they often use a 10-by-10 grid as a model. Dimes and pennies also can be used to represent these numbers. Though not proportional, they are familiar to most students, as is their relative value. Models for thousandths are less familiar. Some teachers use base ten materials, labeling the thousand as one, which makes the small unit a thousandth. However, students may find it difficult to change the value of materials with which they are already familiar. For those who are quite knowledgeable about the metric system, millimeters may be helpful. We suggest using ten 10-by-10 grids and assigning the entire figure the value of one.

Models help students get a sense of the relative sizes of the numbers and to remember the relationships among the various place values. This is essential, because the traditional algorithms for addition and subtraction of decimals require students to recognize that, for example, the number 2.358 can be represented by 2 ones, 3 tenths, 5 hundredths, and 8 thousandths. Or 1 hundredth can be traded for 10 thousandths, for example, resulting in 2 ones, 3 tenths, 4 hundredths, and 18 thousandths.

In the Classroom

A teacher has made a transparency of the *Thousandths Grid* reproducible on page A31 of the appendix and shows it to his students, telling them it has a value of 1. He traces the outline of one of the 10-by-10 arrays within the whole and asks its value. The students readily agree that it is $\frac{1}{10}$, and the teacher records the number as both $\frac{1}{10}$ and *0.1*. Then he runs his finger across the ten squares in the top row of that 10-by-10 array and asks the value of that row. There is a slight pause this time, but then one student suggests it is worth $\frac{1}{100}$, and the rest of the class agrees. The teacher records $\frac{1}{100}$ and *0.01* just below the previous two numbers. Next the teacher points to just one small square and tells the students to talk with a neighbor about the value of the small square and how to record the number as a fraction and a decimal. Once they have identified the value and recorded it as $\frac{1}{1,000}$, they use patterns to determine that the decimal would be written as *0.001*. The teacher points back to the row showing 0.01 and asks, "How many thousandths is this?"

Students reply that it is ten-thousandths. In response to the question "How do you know?" a student comes up and points to the ten individual small squares. Students then show why one-tenth can also be named ten-hundredths and one hundred–thousandths.

Over time, students need a variety of opportunities to make sense of thousandths, such as the following:

- Display a picture of a sign that shows the price of gasoline at a service station and ask students to identify the portion of a dollar that the fraction of a cent represents. Encourage students to note how unit prices in grocery stores usually include a fraction of a cent as well.
- Give each student a copy of the *Thousandths Grid* reproducible and say a number. Their task is to shade the appropriate number of squares to show that number and to write it as a decimal and as a fraction.
- Have students enter a constant function of +0.001 into their calculators. As they make their calculators count, ask questions such as *When will the numbers get one digit shorter? Why does this happen?*
- Show students the back of a meter stick and ask them to estimate lengths such as 181 millimeters, 750 millimeters, and 62 millimeters. Note whether they recognize how small 0.062 of a meter is and if they use benchmark numbers such as 0.5 and 0.75 to help them estimate the other distances.
- Provide a set of clues such as the following and have students figure out the mystery number(s) in the *What's My Number?* reproducible on page A32 of the appendix. Have students practice recognizing nonstandard representations of decimals by filling in the blanks to questions such as the following:

1. I have _____ hundredths and 31 thousandths. I have the number 0.051.
2. I have 2 tenths, 43 hundredths, and 13 thousandths. What number do I have? _____

Meeting Individual Needs

Listen to how students pronounce the names of the decimal places and carefully enunciate these terms yourself. As students are far more familiar with *hundreds* and *thousands*, they may interchange these names with *hundredths* and *thousandths*.

It's important to keep models available to all students. Even those with a strong conceptual base may want to check their ideas with a picture of 1,000 squares, particularly when they are comparing or renaming numbers. Many students may also benefit from having a place-value chart available.

Challenge students and provide them with opportunities to apply the ten-to-one rule across several places by asking such questions as *How many pennies would you have if you had $1,000 in pennies?*

REFERENCE/FURTHER READING

Suh, Jennifer, Chris Johnson, Spenser Jamieson, and Michelle Mills. 2008. "Promoting Decimal Number Sense and Representational Fluency." *Mathematics Teaching in the Middle School* 14 (1): 44–50.

Mathematical Focus

- Convert fractions to decimals.

Potential Challenges and Misconceptions

Many students memorize a procedure for converting fractions to decimals without understanding why they are using that procedure. It is important for students to think critically about why certain fractions are equivalent to specific decimals. Since we operate in a base ten system, it is appropriate to model fractions as decimals on a 10-by-10 grid.

In the Classroom

Before beginning a lesson on converting fractions to decimals, one teacher asks her students to use a 10-by-10 grid to represent the fraction two-fifths. Most of the students provide one of the three representations shown in the figure.

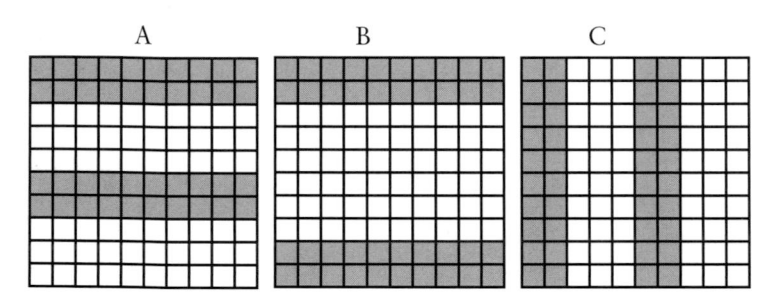

The class discusses the similarities and differences among the representations. The students who used A and C explain that they colored in two squares for every five. The students who provided B explain they colored in two out of the first five rows then started at the bottom and colored in two out of the last five rows.

The teacher asks the students how they might represent the colored squares in the grid numerically. The students all agree they can write the fraction $\frac{40}{100}$. Many of the students simplify the fraction to illustrate $\frac{2}{5} = \frac{40}{100} = 0.40$.

The teacher follows this example by asking the students to show her how they might use the 10-by-10 grid to model the fraction one-eighth. (See figures A–C.)

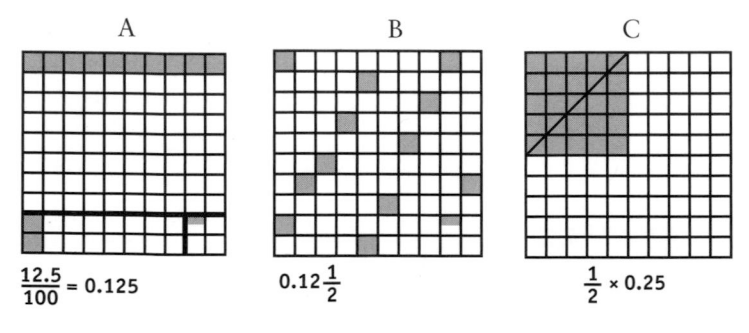

$\frac{12.5}{100} = 0.125$ $0.12\frac{1}{2}$ $\frac{1}{2} \times 0.25$

The students who drew the representation shown in A explain that they counted down eight units, drew a line across, then shaded in the first row. They share that this illustrates one out of eight, but since there were two additional rows, they outlined

eight units in each row and shaded in two squares to define two more eighths. The remaining four squares represented half of the eight they needed. They shaded in one of those squares and gave it a value of one-half. To represent how many squares were shaded, they listed $\frac{12.5}{100}$ squares, or 0.125 squares.

Next the students who used the representation shown in B share their thinking. They simply shaded in one out of every eight squares. When they came to the last column, they explain, they had only one-half of the eight squares they needed, so they shaded in one, which they indicated was one-half. They counted up the number of shaded squares and wrote it as a decimal that included a fraction: $0.12\frac{1}{2}$.

Finally, the student who used the representation shown in C shares that she found one-quarter of the grid, then cut that in half and counted $12\frac{1}{2}$ squares.

After engaging the students in representing a variety of fractions on the hundreds grid, which are included in the *Decimal Grids* reproducible on page A33 of the appendix, the teacher challenges the students to identify an algorithm they can use to check their work. She records the students' thinking on the conjecture board (see figure) before having them check their thinking using a calculator.

> ### Conjecture Board
> *You count up the number of squares by what is in the denominator and you shade in the number shown in the numerator.*
>
> *The denominator tells you how many parts are in the whole. If the denominator is 4, then there are four parts in the whole. The numerator tells how many of the parts are shaded.*

Meeting Individual Needs

For many students, the visual model of the 10-by-10 grid is the key to unlocking a concept that has always been so abstract. Some students need to spend a great deal of time working on the grids before transitioning to the algorithm of dividing the numerator by the denominator. Many students confuse which number is the divisor and which is the dividend when they are converting fractions to decimals. One way to help those students is to have them write the fraction, extend the vinculum (fraction bar), and move the numerator into the dividend. For example:

$$\frac{2}{5\overline{)2.00}}$$

There are some students who can sketch the decimal equivalent as quickly as others complete the algorithm. These students often need to be coaxed to transition to the algorithm.

REFERENCE/FURTHER READING

Suh, Jennifer M., Chris Johnston, Spencer Jamieson, and Michelle Mills. 2008. "Promoting Decimal Number Sense and Representational Fluency." *Mathematics Teaching in the Middle School* 14 (1): 44–50.

Equivalent Values

Mathematical Focus
- Convert fractions to decimals.
- Compare the values of decimals whose fractional equivalents have numerators that are one less than the denominators (e.g., three-fourths).

Potential Challenges and Misconceptions
Reliance on algorithms for finding decimal values equivalent to fractional values deprives students of the reasoning that they need to become more sophisticated with rational numbers. Developing proportional reasoning requires students to think relatively (that is, to think about a quantity in relation to other quantities), which includes a multiplicative process. This compares with their thinking absolutely, which includes the additive process to which they are accustomed. It is in grades five and six that most students make this transition. This means that as students compare a list of fractions, such as $\frac{2}{3}$, $\frac{4}{6}$, $\frac{6}{9}$, and $\frac{8}{12}$, you should encourage them to describe the pattern in terms of the multiplicative identity $\frac{2}{3} \times \frac{2}{2}$ (which has a value of 1) $= \frac{4}{6}$. Since they are multiplying by 1, the value of the fraction does not change, but rather the numerator and denominator grow by a scale factor of 2. Teachers who promote this language, rather than comments such as *the numerator adds two and the denominator adds three each time*, are providing an environment that fosters proportional reasoning.

In the Classroom
As students progress through the grades, the basic facts they should know change. It is extremely helpful for students to know, or at the very least recognize, the decimal equivalents for commonly used fractions. Students who can reason through the relation of fractions to benchmark fractions, such as knowing that since $\frac{1}{8}$ is $\frac{1}{2}$ of $\frac{1}{4}$, the decimal equivalent is $\frac{1}{2}$ of 0.25, or 0.125, have an easier time making sense of problem situations that require a knowledge of fractions and decimals. The following are some activities that help build that understanding.

- Provide each student with a table on which he or she must use the given values and reason through to find the missing values. Do not allow students to use calculators, because they can find these values by halving, doubling, or tripling or by adding two known values.

Benchmark Fraction	Benchmark Decimal
$\frac{3}{4}$	
$\frac{1}{2}$	0.50
$\frac{1}{4}$	
	0.125
$\frac{3}{8}$	
	0.625
$\frac{7}{8}$	

- *Equivalent Fractions and Decimals:* On heavy stock, make copies of the *Equivalent Fractions and Decimals Cards* reproducible on page A34 of the appendix and cut out the cards. Give a set of cards to each pair of students. They shuffle the cards and arrange them facedown in a rectangular array. The students alternate turning over two cards at a time, trying to match a fraction value with its decimal equivalent. If a student makes a match, she keeps the pair of cards. If there is no match, the student turns both cards facedown and the other player takes a turn. The object is to match as many pairs as possible.

- Have students sit in groups of six or eight. Give them one calculator to share, which they pass among themselves. The first person inputs $\frac{1}{2}$ and finds the decimal equivalent. One student records the fraction and the decimal equivalent on easel-size paper or on an individual-size whiteboard. The student passes the calculator to the student on his left. This student inputs the fraction $\frac{2}{3}$, but before she presses the equal sign, the students record the fraction and a predicted decimal equivalent on individual recording sheets. The student with the calculator presses the equal sign and shares the decimal equivalent. This student passes the calculator to the left and the next student inputs the fraction $\frac{3}{4}$, but before he presses the equal sign, the students record the fraction and a predicted decimal equivalent on individual recording sheets. The student with the calculator presses the equal sign and shares the decimal equivalent. This continues as the students input fractions. After all students have a chance to input a fraction, the students review the list they made and share any patterns they see. The class discusses the relationship between the value of the fraction and its decimal equivalent as well as strategies for mental computation. They agree that the change in the decimal equivalents lessens as the pattern continues as the relative difference between the numerator and denominator decreases.

Meeting Individual Needs
Some students benefit from returning to the visual model to convert fractions to decimals. It is helpful to provide these students with hundreds grids and ask them to shade in the number of squares that represents a particular fraction.

REFERENCE/FURTHER READING
Gawronski, Jane, Marthe Craig, Mary Eich, and Kim Morris. 2005. *Mathematics Assessment Sampler, Grades 3–5: Items Aligned with NCTM's Principles and Standards for School Mathematics.* Reston, VA: National Council of Teachers of Mathematics.

Mathematical Focus

- Estimate decimals.
- Use estimation to identify the range of accepted values in problem solving.

Potential Challenges and Misconceptions

"Students' number sense is enhanced when they are encouraged to use numbers in real contexts and to estimate quantities in different mathematical settings" (Welchman 1999, 240). Many students and teachers alike simplify decimals and eliminate 0s that are located at the end of a number; for example, they write 2 rather than 2.0. The common misconception is that the 0 can be dropped because it does not change the value. However, 2.0 is read as *two and zero tenths* and is precise to the nearest tenth. The range of values represented by 2.0 are all those between 1.95 and 2.4. Including 0s at the end of a decimal indicates to what place value the measurement is accurate. If the number were written as 2.00, the range of values it would represent would be those between 1.995 and 2.004. When students are estimating, it is helpful for them to include the information that tells to how many places the estimate is precise. The number 2 is less precise than the number 2.0, which is less precise than the number 2.00, and so on.

In the Classroom

Estimation is one area in which students typically show a wide range of understanding. Many think to estimate means to compute an answer and then round it. Other students think it means to drop all the digits that follow the place value to which they are estimating.

Range questions, such as those that follow, can help you uncover student strengths and misconceptions:

- *Name two ways you can estimate the sum of 3.57 + 7.20.*
- *Tim estimated the difference between 0.39 and 0.32 as 0.7. Is he correct? If not, explain how you could help him see his error.*
- *Approximate the sum of 7.78 + 26.597.*
- *Billy gave Mr. McDonald a $20 bill to pay for a purchase of $11.48. Mr. McDonald gave Billy back one $5 bill, four $1 bills, two quarters, and two pennies. Did Billy receive the correct change? How do you know?*
- *Estimate the difference between 5.187 and 0.48.*

After listening to the students' explanations, it is appropriate to formalize the strategies the students use when estimating sums and differences. Since this teacher recognizes it is far more beneficial for the students to articulate strategies for estimation than for her to tell them what works, she challenges them to define some guidelines for estimating. She records their thinking on the conjecture board. (See figure.)

Conjectures for Estimating Sums and Differences

- *Just use the front end of the number and add or subtract.*
- *Look at the decimal in the tenths place and use that to round up or leave the number in the units place alone and add or subtract the units.*
- *Look at the number to the right of the front-end number. If that is between 5 and 9, round the front number up and add or subtract the front number.*

Notice that each of the conjectures refers to the front-end number (rounding a number based upon the number in the leftmost place) or using just the tenths place if decimals are included. The teacher asks the students whether any of their conjectures will work if they have to find the difference to the nearest hundredth between 0.045 and 0.027. She instructs the students to try each of the conjectures and to revise the one that comes closest to what they need to do. (See figure.)

Revised Conjectures for Estimating Sums and Differences

- *Look at the digit to the right of the place to which you are rounding. If that is between 0 and 4, leave the digit in the place to which you are rounding alone. If the digit to the right is between 5 and 9, round up. Drop the rest of the digits to the right. Add or subtract.*

Moira: Is this always true?
Teacher: Only if the computation is context free.

Meeting Individual Needs

Many students need practice with estimating, but some students need greater challenges. These students should engage in problem solving. Sample problems are included in the *Decimals and Problem Solving* reproducible on page A35 of the appendix.

For real-world estimating, bring in a collection of shopping receipts and challenge the students to estimate the total of the bills to the nearest dollar.

REFERENCES/FURTHER READING

Drum, Randal, and Wesley Petty Jr. 2000. "2 Is Not the Same as 2.0." *Mathematics Teaching in the Middle School* 6 (1): 34–38.

Glasgow, Robert, Gay Ragan, Wanda M. Fields, Robert Reys, and Deanna Wasman. 2000. "The Decimal Dilemma." *Teaching Children Mathematics* 7 (2): 89–93.

Welchman, Rosamond. 1999. "What Is Your Millennial Age?" *Teaching Children Mathematics* 6 (4): 240–42.

Adding and Subtracting Decimals

Mathematical Focus

- Add and subtract decimals.

Potential Challenges and Misconceptions

Katherine Irwin (2001) interviewed eighty-four students from New Zealand and documented these commonly held misconceptions about decimal fractions:

- Longer decimals are necessarily larger.
- Longer decimals are necessarily smaller.
- Putting a zero at the end of a decimal number makes it ten times as large.
- Decimals act as a decorative dot.
- When you do something to one side of the dot, you also do it to the other side (e.g., 2.5 + 1 = 3.6).
- Decimal fractions are "below zero," or negative, numbers.
- Place-value columns include "oneths" to the right of the decimal point.
- One-hundredth is written *0.100*.
- One-fourth can be written either as *0.4* or as *0.25*.

It is important that teachers continuously check on their students' understanding of decimals to ensure they do not hold on to these common misconceptions.

In the Classroom

One teacher challenges her students to solve the following problem:

> *What is the sum of 23.7, 6.912, and 0.14?*

As the students work on finding the sum, the teacher walks around, listening to the students discuss how they should line up the numbers.

Chrissy: What if we estimate the sum before we add?
Andy: Before we do that, we should write the problem up and down.
Mandy: But that's the problem—how do we line up the numbers? . . . Let's all try and see if we agree.

The students write the addends vertically, coming up with two different alignments.

23.7		23.7
6.912		6.912
0.14		0.14

They wonder how they can determine the correct alignment. Chrissy suggests they add the values first, then check the sum using a calculator. They do so and obtain the following results.

23.7		23.7
6.912		6.912
0.14		0.14
9.422		30.752

Before giving them permission to check their results with a calculator, the teacher asks them to predict which sum is correct and to explain their thinking. Some of the students explain they aligned the front-end digits and added. Other students say they know the answer has to be closer to thirty since they are adding almost twenty-four to seven. They also notice the decimal points are aligned in the second version. After checking the answer with the calculator, the students examine the differences between their two vertical examples and make a conjecture for adding decimals. (See figure.)

Conjectures for Adding Decimals

- *Add zeros to all numbers so all the numbers have the same number of places. Line up the decimal points. Add the numbers.*
- *Line up the decimal point and add the numbers.*
- *Line up the decimal points, then add zeros as placeholders. Add the numbers.*

Next the teacher asks the students if they could use their conjectures for subtraction. She asks them to compute $7 - 2.4578$ using their conjectures. Some students are confused because there is no decimal point in the first addend.

Luke: We didn't do any like this. The 7 doesn't have a decimal point.
Kenny: Just add 0s; then you can subtract.
Sabrina: You can't just add 0s. That would change the 7 to 70, 700, 7,000, 70,000, and those numbers are much bigger than 7. You have to put in a decimal point and write 7.0000 so the value doesn't change.

After this discussion on the placement of the decimal point and the 0s, the group continues on and subtracts correctly. The students check their answer with their calculator.

Finally, the teacher gives them the *Problem Solving* reproducible on page A36 of the appendix for further practice.

Meeting Individual Needs

Many students struggle when they are asked to subtract decimal values from whole numbers. An effective way of engaging students in doing this subtraction is to use play money. Provide these students practice with subtracting cents from dollar-bill values, such as $0.37 from a $5.00 bill. It is helpful for some of these students to actually make change as they work toward solidifying their understanding of subtracting decimals from whole numbers. Many may benefit from counting up, as clerks often do in a store. For example: $0.37 + **$0.03** = $0.40; $0.40 + **$0.10** = $0.50; $0.50 + **$0.50** = $1.00; $1.00 + **$4.00** = $5.00; therefore, the amount of change is $4.63.

REFERENCES/FURTHER READING

Irwin, Katherine. 2001. "Using Everyday Knowledge of Decimals to Enhance Understanding." *Journal for Research in Mathematics Education* 32 (4): 399–420.

National Center for Educational Statistics. 2007. *TIMSS 8 Mathematics Items*. http://nces.ed.gov/TIMSS/pdf/TIMSS8_Math_Items.pdf.

Multiplying Decimals with Arrays

Mathematical Focus
- Multiply decimals using a Cartesian coordinate plane.

Potential Challenges and Misconceptions
Since we deal with a decimal number system, it is important that students understand how decimals operate. Students frequently have difficulty determining what to do with the decimal point when they multiply with decimals. Too often they are told to count the number of decimal places in the factors and move the decimal that number of places to the left in the product. This unfortunately does not engender understanding. Students often do not understand that if a whole number is multiplied by a decimal, the product will be less than the larger factor. Providing a visual representation is an effective way to allow students to see what happens in the multiplication of decimals.

In the Classroom
Before discussing any procedures for multiplying decimals, one teacher gives her students a grid with both the *x*- and *y*-axes labeled in tenths. See the *Decimal Multiplication Grids* reproducible on page A37 of the appendix. She asks her students to predict the product they would get if they multiplied 1×0.1. (These students have previous experience with the area model of multiplication, which is discussed in "Multiplying Fractions with Arrays.")

Alex begins the discussion. "I predict the product is ten because there will be ten squares filled in."

Martha explains, "I predict the product is less than one whole because when we multiplied one whole by a fraction, the product was less than one. So, I think the answer is one-tenth."

Katie adds, "I agree with Martha. We discovered when you multiply a whole by a part of a whole, the product is less than the whole. So, I say one-tenth."

After recording the predictions on the conjecture board, the teacher directs the students to illustrate the representation on the grids and to discuss in small groups what the representation means. (See figure below on left.)

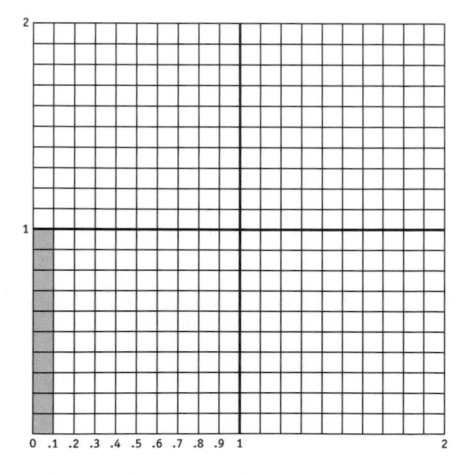

As the teacher walks around to each group, she hears one group struggling to understand why the product is not ten, if ten units are shaded. She asks the group to shade the product of 1×1.

Then she asks them to discuss how the product of 1×1 is similar to and different from the product of 1×0.1.

Jeremy says, "I counted one hundred squares when I multiplied one by one. I thought there would only be one since one times one equals one."

Then Patrick explains, "I get it. The grid shows that there are ten decimal values named between zero and one, so one-tenth takes up ten squares, but that is a lot less than the number of squares there are in one whole. We could write the product like a fraction, ten-hundredths."

Jeremy replies, "If we simplified the fraction, we'd get one-tenth, which is what Martha said. I wonder what we'd get if we multiplied one-tenth by one-tenth?"

This group decides to try to find the product of 0.1×0.1. The added decimal values to the grid and discover the answer to their question is 0.01. (See figure.)

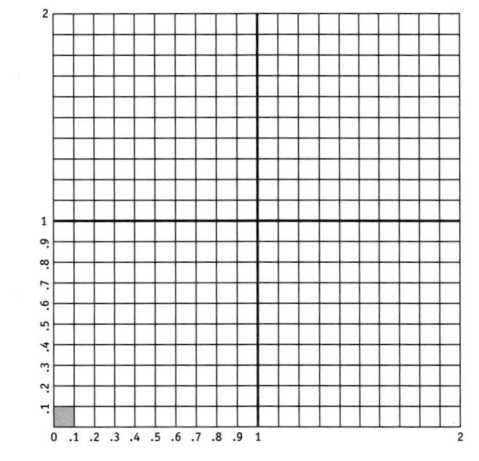

Next the teacher asks the class to explore different multiplication examples and to record both the factors and the product for each in a table. (See the *Decimal Multiplication Tables* reproducible on page A38 of the appendix.) She also challenges the students to identify any patterns they notice and to see if they can determine what is happening mathematically without using the grids.

After making their conjectures, the students test them by multiplying tenths times hundredths and hundredths times hundredths.

Meeting Individual Needs
Some students may already know the rule for multiplying with decimals. If so, it is important for them to be able to explain why it works. These students benefit more from the grids than the tables. Many students, especially those who prefer a visual representation, do best when they use the grids and tables together. Some students need to use the grids for a longer period of time than others. It might help some students if the table and grid are presented on one sheet. Provide students the option of using a graphic organizer designed to help them organize their thinking and their work.

REFERENCE/FURTHER READING
Van de Walle, John, Karen Karp, and Jennifer Bay-Williams. 2010. *Elementary and Middle School Mathematics: Teaching Developmentally.* 7th ed. New York: Pearson Education.

Dividing Decimals

A39,A40

Mathematical Focus
- Divide decimals using a multiplication menu.

Potential Challenges and Misconceptions
Most students struggle with division of whole numbers and are even more confused when decimals are involved. Before students can understand decimal division, it is important for them to be proficient with division of whole numbers. Students also need a lot of varied problems and computations with decimals as they build that proficiency.

In the Classroom
One teacher asks her students to help her determine how many students have paid for their snacks. Each snack costs $0.45, and the teacher has collected $10.35. Students work in small groups to solve the problem.

One group begins by setting up a division problem. The students discuss the fact that they need to determine how many groups of $0.45 are in $10.35, and all agree that if they divide $10.35 by $0.45, they will know how many students have paid. Because they are comfortable with using a multiplication menu, they set up a menu next to their division problem (see figure).

$$0.45 \overline{)10.35}$$

Multiplication Menu
$1 \times 0.45 = 0.45$
$10 \times 0.45 = 4.5$
$5 \times 0.45 = 2.25$
$20 \times 0.45 = 9.0$
$25 \times 0.45 = 11.25$ this is too large
$2 \times 0.45 = .90$
$3 \times 0.45 = 1.35$
$23 \times 0.45 = 10.35$

$$0.45 \overline{)10.35} \quad 23$$

The students use a doubling and halving strategy combined with an addition strategy. They add the multipliers and the product to find additional values.

Another group divides the numbers without using a decimal multiplication menu. The first thing these students agree upon is that they do not like working with decimals. They decide to see what would happen if they used equivalent nondecimal values. They begin by making a chart.

Dividend	Divisor	Quotient
1	1	1
1	0.1	10
10	1	10
1	0.01	100
100	1	100

Based on their table, they make a conjecture that if you multiply the divisor and the dividend by the same multiple of ten, you get the same answer as you would if you divided with decimals. They apply this strategy to the problem.

$$0.45 \overline{)10.35} \text{ is the same as } 45 \overline{)1035}$$
$$\begin{array}{r} 3 \\ 20 \\ \hline 900 \\ 135 \\ 135 \\ \hline 0 \end{array}$$

23 students paid

Multiplication Menu
$1 \times 45 = 45$
$10 \times 45 = 450$
$20 \times 45 = 900$
$5 \times 45 = 225$
$25 \times 45 = 1,125$ which is too big
$23 \times 45 = 1,035$

Next, the teacher asks her students to help her figure out the miles per gallon her car gets. She explains that she drove 237.75 miles and put 15.5 gallons of gas in her car. Before she sends them off to work on the actual mileage, she asks the students to predict how many miles per gallon they think she got. She records the predictions, which range from 20 to 25 miles per gallon, on the conjecture board.

The students report out their work after spending time working in groups to calculate the number of miles per gallon. Tony reports:

> My group looked at the 237.75 and 15.5 and decided to estimate first. We figured that if we rounded we could see how many times 16 gallons went into 238 miles. We knew it would be less than 20 and more than 10, since 16 times 20 equals 320 and 16 times 10 equals 160. We tried 15 and got 160 plus 80 equals 240, so we think the car got just under 15 miles per gallon.
>
> We found that the car got between 15.3 and 15.4 miles per gallon. We also think a close estimate is all we need to know.

The class discusses Tony's strategy. Other students suggest that Tony should have said the car would get more than 15 miles per gallon to make up for rounding the values.

The class continues to work on problems like this. Similar problems are included in the *More Problems with Decimals* reproducible on page A39 of the appendix. For students struggling with the decimal point, try *Where Does the Decimal Go?* on page A40 of the appendix.

Meeting Individual Needs
Some students will come to class having been told by a parent or sibling that all you do when you divide with decimals is move the decimal point to the right in the divisor to turn it into a whole number and then move the decimal in the dividend the same number of places. These students should be challenged to explain why this method works. Other students may need more support with setting up a multiplication menu and understanding the importance of placing the decimal in the appropriate location. They may even benefit from doing more estimation with decimals before engaging in formal computations that require an exact answer.

REFERENCE/FURTHER READING
Van de Walle, John, Karen Karp, and Jennifer Bay-Williams. 2010. *Elementary and Middle School Mathematics: Teaching Developmentally.* 7th ed. New York: Pearson Education.

Mathematical Focus

- Use ratio as a rate.
- Apply ratio to rate problems.
- Develop the use of ratio tables.

Potential Misconceptions and Challenges

In addition to the confusion students often experience with understanding the difference between fractions and ratios, they also find it difficult to understand how ratios may be used to express a rate. Think about a rate as a means of envisioning a wide range of circumstances where all the quantities are related in some way (Lamon 1999, 204). Rates are used to indicate the relation between two separate units of measure connected by the term *per*. For instance, a car may get 23 miles per gallon, or a sale of six oranges for $1.69 can be simplified to one orange for $0.28. When a rate is simplified to the cost of a unit, we usually refer to it as the *unit rate*.

To add to the confusion, rates can be constant or they may vary. Think about the number of inches in a foot, feet in a yard, and feet in a mile, for instance: the rate is always the same, or is constant. Now think about how fast you ride your bicycle, or how fast you complete your homework, or how hard it rains: the rates vary depending on a variety of circumstances. Are you riding up a hill or down a hill? Are you concentrating on getting your homework done quickly or are you doodling, talking on the phone, or having trouble with the work? Is it a torrential downpour or a drizzling rain?

Rates can also be represented as a single value when they are expressed as a quotient. An example might be your pulse, which is usually given as a single number (e.g., 70), or your body mass index, which is also expressed as a single number (e.g., 24), despite the fact that the first represents a ratio of beats per minute and the second, a ratio of your height to your weight, or pounds per inch.

As these are subtle yet complex differences, it is very clear why so many teachers struggle with how and when to teach them. However, rate is an important prealgebra concept that can be successfully developed using rate tables.

In the Classroom

A most effective strategy for engaging students with rates is through problem solving. One teacher poses the following question to her class.

> Our class is responsible for making the hot chocolate for the winter festival. We want the hot chocolate to be rich and chocolatey. How much milk and how much chocolate powder do you think will make the tastiest drink?

She provides each group of students a measuring cup, chocolate powder, and milk. She encourages them to think individually about the problem before discussing their ideas in the group. After an allotted period of time, she records their comments on the board, including the following:

> We need to know how many people will attend.
> We need to know how much hot chocolate each person will drink.

> We need to figure out if we should put as much chocolate as milk in the mixture.
> We know we need a lot more milk than chocolate powder.
> We can make different mixtures and taste them.

After all the groups have a chance to share their thinking, she sends the students to their work areas to begin solving the problem. Each workstation has measuring spoons, a pitcher, and some empty glasses. The students begin experimenting with the mixture and the teacher prompts them to record all their measurements in their notebooks. After the allotted time, the students report their findings. They agree that a ratio of 2 tablespoons of chocolate to 3 cups of milk works well. Their next challenge is to figure out how much milk and chocolate they would need to serve one cup each to 250 people. Each group reports its strategy and solution. For example:

- *Fiona:* Our group thought it would be best to make a table.

Tablespoons of chocolate	2	4	6	8	10	20	40	80	160	168
Cups of milk	3	6	9	12	15	30	60	120	240	252

We started with a ratio of $\frac{2}{3}$ and multiplied it by 1 over and over. First 1 equaled $\frac{2}{2}$, then $\frac{3}{3}$, $\frac{4}{4}$, then $\frac{5}{5}$. This took a long time, so we multiplied $\frac{10}{10}$, then $\frac{20}{20}$, then $\frac{40}{40}$. Then we multiplied $\frac{80}{120}$ by $\frac{2}{2}$ to get to 240 cups. We needed 250 cups, so we added $\frac{8}{12}$ for a total of 252 cups of milk and 168 tablespoons of chocolate.

- *Lucas:* Our group also started with a table. But we saw that we were making equivalent ratios, so we figured we needed to know how many times 3 cups of milk fit into 250 cups. We divided 250 by 3 and got $83\frac{1}{3}$. Then we multiplied 2 by $83\frac{1}{3}$ because for every 3 cups of milk, we need 2 tablespoons of chocolate, and got $166\frac{2}{3}$. We rounded that to 167 tablespoons of chocolate with 250 cups of milk.

To end this lesson, the teacher has students work on the *Solving Problems with Rates* reproducible on page A41 of the appendix.

Meeting Individual Needs

Some students are able to transition from the ratio table to a more abstract representation sooner than others. These students respond well to setting up proportions and finding the scale factor to use in finding missing values. Lucas' group described this scale factor process very eloquently while at the same time illustrating that ratios also act as operators. His group divided by the denominator and multiplied by the numerator.

REFERENCE/FURTHER READING

Lamon, Susan. 1999. *Teaching Fractions and Ratios for Understanding: Essential Content Knowledge and Instructional Strategies for Teachers.* Mahwah, NJ: Erlbaum.

APPENDIX

Name: Date:

Millions in My Life

I have seen 1,000,000:	I have eaten 1,000,000:	I have done these activities at least 1,000,000 times:
One million of these things would fit in our classroom:	Counting to 1,000,000 would take me:	If I had $1,000,000, I would:

Billions

1. How many millions are there in a billion?

2. How long is a billion seconds?

3. What would you not want to have a billion of?

4. What examples would you give to someone who wanted to know just how big a billion was?

Direction Cards

Make the **greatest** number possible.

Make the **least** number possible.

Make the **greatest** sum.

Make the **least** sum.

Direction Cards

Make the **greatest** difference.

Make the **least** difference.

Make the **greatest** product.

Make the **least** product.

Digit Cards

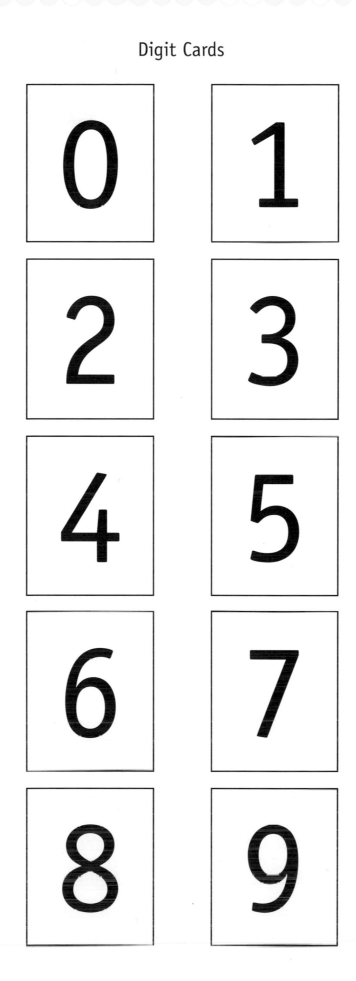

Name: Date:

Find the missing seven-digit number.

- *Double 16. Divide the result by 8. Write the answer in the* tens *place.*

- *Multiply 6 by 4. Divide the result by 3. Write the answer in the* ten thousands *place.*

- *The digit in the* millions *place is $\frac{1}{2}$ the digit in the* tens *place.*

- *Multiply the digit in the* millions *place by 9. Divide the result by 3. Write the answer in the* ones *place.*

- *Double 25. Divide the result by 10. Write the answer in the* hundred thousands *place.*

- *Multiply the digit in the* ones *place by the digit in the* ten thousands *place. Subtract the product of 9 times 5 from the result. Write the answer in the* hundreds *place.*

- *Add the digit in the* millions *place to the digit in the* hundred thousands *place. Write the answer in the* thousands *place.*

Make up a puzzle using place value clues. Challenge a classmate to solve your puzzle.

Name: Date:

Place your starting number in the first starburst and then complete the calculations until you reach the end. What do you notice?

+ 5   × 2   − 4   ÷ 2   − 3   + 4   × 6   + 9   ÷ 3   − 11   ÷ 2   + 8   × 4   − 12   ÷ 2   − 10   ÷ 2   + 7   − 5   × 6   ÷ 3   − 4   ÷ 2

End

SIEVE OF ERATOSTHENES

Name: Date:

1. Cross out the number 1.

2. Circle the number 2, then draw a line through any number that is a multiple of 2 and write *2* in that box.

3. Circle the number 3, then draw a line through any number that is a multiple of 3 and write *3* in that box.

4. Circle the number 5, then draw a line through any number that is a multiple of 5 and write *5* in that box.

5. Circle the number 7, then draw a line through any number that is a multiple of 7 and write *7* in that box.

1	2	3	4	5	6	7	8	9	10
11	12	13	14	15	16	17	18	19	20
21	22	23	24	25	26	27	28	29	30
31	32	33	34	35	36	37	38	39	40
41	42	43	44	45	46	47	48	49	50
51	52	53	54	55	56	57	58	59	60
61	62	63	64	65	66	67	68	69	70
71	72	73	74	75	76	77	78	79	80
81	82	83	84	85	86	87	88	89	90
91	92	93	94	95	96	97	98	99	100

Zeroing in on Number and Operations: Key Ideas and Common Misconceptions, Grades 5–6 by Anne Collins and Linda Dacey. Copyright © 2010. Stenhouse Publishers.

Name: Date:

A teacher places multiple copies of the following shapes in a bag.

circle   square   cross   triangle   hexagon

Then the teacher pulls out a few shapes and finds the product of their values.

1. If the product is **300**, how many shapes did the teacher pull from the bag? What are the values of the shapes pulled from the bag? Justify your answer.

2. If the product is **693**, how many shapes did the teacher pull from the bag? What are the values of the shapes pulled from the bag? Justify your answer.

3. If the product is **2,205**, how many shapes did the teacher pull from the bag? What are the values of the shapes pulled from the bag? Justify your answer.

4. If the product is **53,361**, how many shapes did the teacher pull from the bag? What are the values of the shapes pulled from the bag? Justify your answer.

Name: Date:

Solve the following problems. Complete a multiplication menu to support your solution for each problem.

1. Zachary is putting his 675 baseball cards in an album. He fills in a total of 45 pages. How many cards are in each page? Justify your answer.

2. Shannon saves $38 per week. At this rate, in how many weeks will she have $874? Justify your answer.

3. You have 351 stickers. You want to give each of your friends 13 stickers since that is your favorite number. How many friends are going to get stickers? Justify your answer.

Name: Date:

Find the quotient for:

Record Your Steps Here	Make a Drawing of Your Steps	Use Words to Explain Your Steps

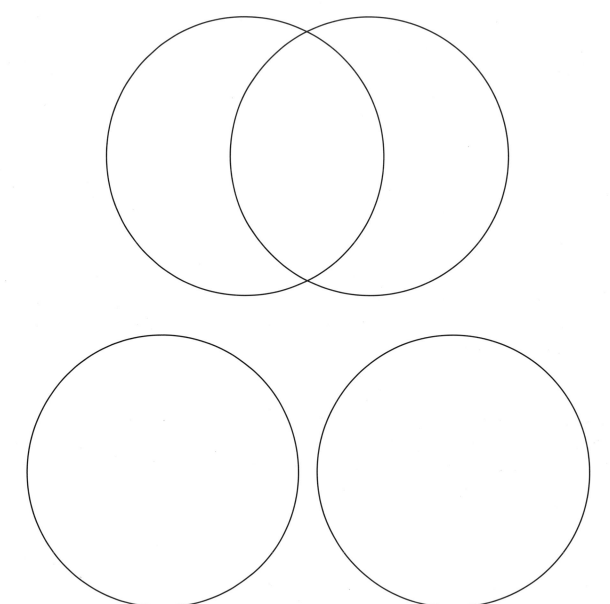

VENN DIAGRAM

Name: Date:

1. The Powder Puffs have soccer practice every three days, weekends included. Play practice is every fourth day, weekends included. Michele is a Powder Puff, has the lead in the play, and also has to babysit her little sister every five days. If all three commitments begin October 1, when is the next time Michele will have all activities on the same day?

2. Jaden has three pieces of licorice lace he wants to share with his friends. One is 42 cm long, a second is 49 cm long, and the third is 63 cm long. He wants to cut equal-length pieces from each of his laces without wasting any licorice and then give one piece to each of his friends. What is the longest possible piece he can cut from each of the laces of licorice? How many pieces will Jaden have to share?

3. Mr. Sullivan is making a mosaic that will be 16 feet by 24 feet. He wants to use congruent tiles. What is the size of the largest square tile he can use?

4. The high school radio station is giving away free tickets to a concert. It will give a free ticket to every 4th and 6th middle school caller. It will also give a free limo ride to every 10th middle school caller. Which caller will be the first to receive a free ticket and a limo ride to the concert?

5. There are 50 girls and 30 boys interested in performing in the school's production of *Riverdance*. Ms. Ima Dancer wants the same number and same gender of students in each row. What is the maximum number of students she can have in each row?

Name: Date:

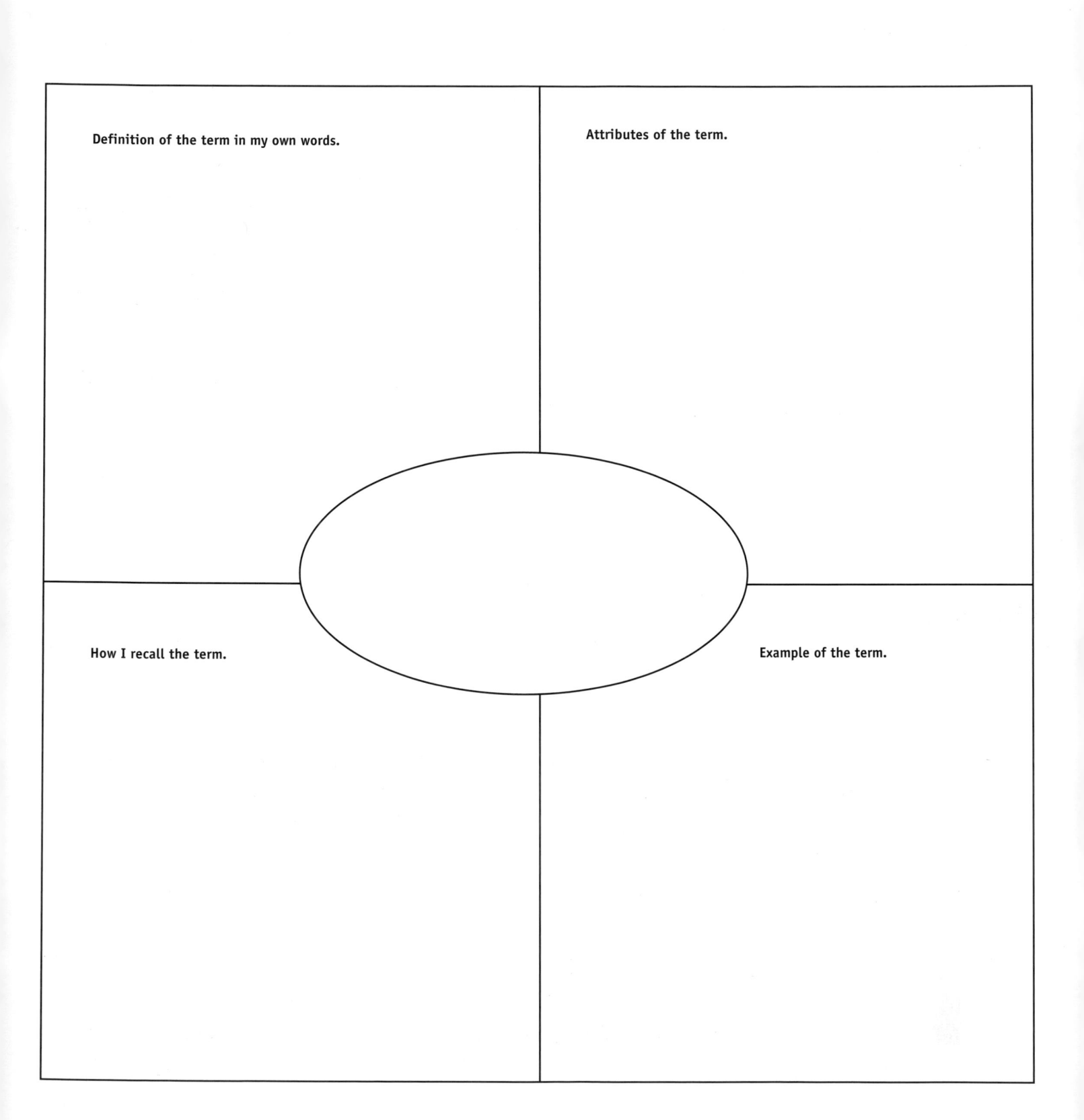

Definition of the term in my own words.

Attributes of the term.

How I recall the term.

Example of the term.

Name: Date:

1. Auntie Mim is baking cookies for her son and his friends. If the 4 boys share 17 cookies equally, how many cookies will each boy receive?

2. A bookstore sold 3,200 books for a total of $52,800. What is the average cost of a book?

3. Grade six teachers want to divide 187 students into teams for field day. They realize that the total number of students is a prime number. What should the teachers do?

4. All the middle schools in the city of Springfield are taking a trip to Washington, DC. There are 2,368 people going on the trip. Each bus holds 38 people. How many buses does the district need for people taking the trip?

5. José is packaging goodies for a school fair. He has a total of 2,457 goodies that he can place into paper bags. If he places exactly 24 goodies in each bag, how many bags of goodies will he have to share?

6. Grandpa Brown is giving each of his 16 grandchildren an equal share of the $354 he won. How much money will each grandchild receive?

7. Use the numbers 110 and 4 in four different problems so that each problem does something different with the remainder.

   a. round the quotient up

   b. represent the remainder as a decimal

   c. ignore the remainder

   d. represent the remainder as a fraction

Game Goal: Be the first player to color four quotients in a row, column, or diagonal.

This is a game for two players. You need this game sheet and two crayons or markers of different colors.

1. Take turns. On each turn, choose one number from A and one number from B.

2. Estimate the quotient for A ÷ B.

3. Color in the estimated quotient on the game board.

4. Continue playing until one player gets four quotients in a row, column, or diagonal.

A
5,420
1,350
10,000
27,450

B
48
237
97
120

100	42	14	120
230	55	12	6
28	5	275	200
25	140	50	45

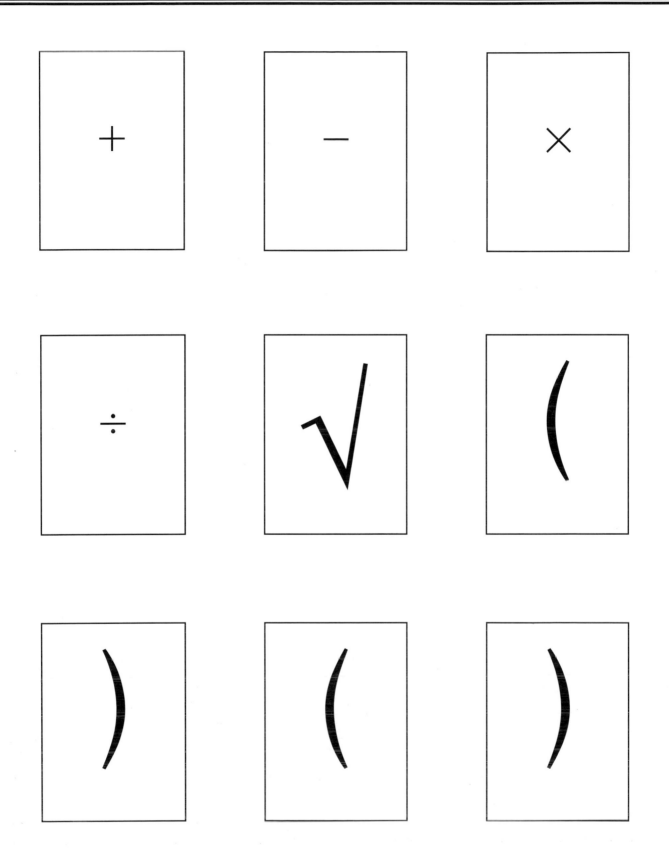

Name: Date:

Can you make the numbers 1–30 just using the operators $+$, $-$, $\times$, and $\div$; parentheses ( ); exponents; square roots; factorials ! and four 4s?

4	4	4	4	= 1	4	4	4	4	= 11	4	4	4	4	= 21
4	4	4	4	= 2	4	4	4	4	= 12	4	4	4	4	= 22
4	4	4	4	= 3	4	4	4	4	= 13	4	4	4	4	= 23
4	4	4	4	= 4	4	4	4	4	= 14	4	4	4	4	= 24
4	4	4	4	= 5	4	4	4	4	= 15	4	4	4	4	= 25
4	4	4	4	= 6	4	4	4	4	= 16	4	4	4	4	= 26
4	4	4	4	= 7	4	4	4	4	= 17	4	4	4	4	= 27
4	4	4	4	= 8	4	4	4	4	= 18	4	4	4	4	= 28
4	4	4	4	= 9	4	4	4	4	= 19	4	4	4	4	= 29
4	4	4	4	= 10	4	4	4	4	= 20	4	4	4	4	= 30

$\frac{1}{2}$	$\frac{1}{3}$	$\frac{1}{4}$	$\frac{1}{6}$	$\frac{1}{8}$
$\frac{2}{3}$	$\frac{2}{4}$	$\frac{2}{6}$	$\frac{2}{8}$	$\frac{3}{4}$
$\frac{3}{6}$	$\frac{3}{8}$	$\frac{4}{8}$	$\frac{5}{8}$	$\frac{7}{8}$

COMPARING FRACTIONS CARDS

$\frac{13}{16}$	$\frac{15}{16}$	$\frac{7}{12}$	$\frac{8}{9}$
$\frac{21}{24}$	$\frac{11}{15}$	$\frac{7}{15}$	$\frac{5}{12}$
$\frac{7}{16}$	$\frac{19}{24}$	$\frac{16}{24}$	$\frac{18}{24}$

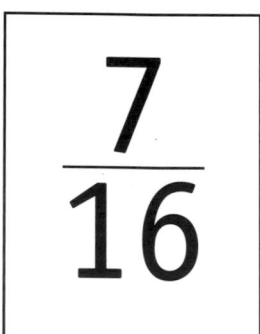

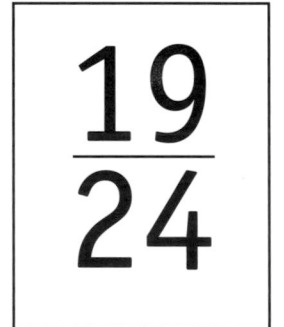

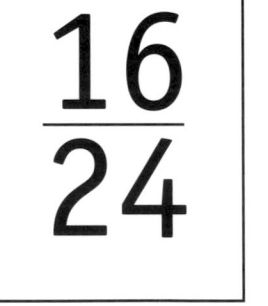

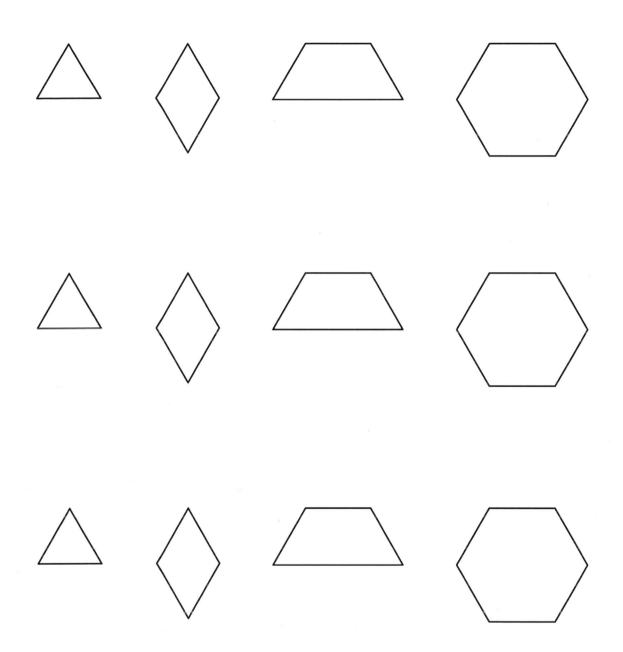

Name: Date:

1. Write a number sentence for the following.

$$\diamond + \bigtriangledown = \bigotimes$$

2. Build a model and complete the following number sentence.

$\frac{1}{2} - \frac{1}{6} = ?$

3. If $\triangle$ equals $\frac{1}{2}$ of a unit, what is the whole?

4. Donovan built the following model and started a number sentence. Help Donovan finish his number sentence.

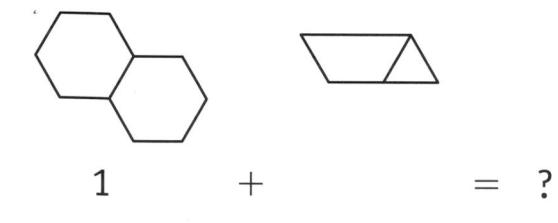

   1   +   =   ?

PROBLEMS WITH FRACTIONS

Name: Date:

1. Danielle made a special snack to take with her on a camping trip. She combined $\frac{1}{3}$ cup of almonds, $\frac{1}{6}$ cup of raisins, $\frac{1}{4}$ cup of chocolate bits, and 1 cup of pretzels. How many cups of her special snack did she make? Justify your answer.

2. Marcus mixed $\frac{5}{8}$ cups of red paint with $2\frac{1}{3}$ cups of white paint. Does he have enough to make the 3 cups of paint his group needs to finish its project? Justify your answer.

3. During their summer vacation, Pete and Manny walk almost everywhere they go. Each week they walk 35 miles. On Monday they walk $4\frac{5}{8}$ miles. On Tuesday they walk $6\frac{1}{2}$ miles. On Wednesday they walk $8\frac{5}{8}$ miles. On Thursday they walk $11\frac{1}{8}$ miles. How many miles do they have to walk on Friday to make their 35 miles?

Zeroing in on Number and Operations: Key Ideas and Common Misconceptions, Grades 5–6 by Anne Collins and Linda Dacey. Copyright © 2010. Stenhouse Publishers.

Make a drawing to model each expression and then write the product.

a. $8 \times \frac{1}{3}$

b. $3 \times 2\frac{1}{6}$

c. $2\frac{1}{2} \times \frac{1}{3}$

d. $3\frac{1}{3} \times 1\frac{1}{2}$

Name: _____   Date: _____

1. Draw a picture to model $2\frac{1}{2} \div \frac{1}{6}$ and write the quotient.

2. Chris made the following model to find $4\frac{1}{3} \div \frac{1}{2}$.

Chris counted the halves and decided the quotient was $8\frac{1}{3}$. Is Chris correct? Why do you think so?

3. Give the missing numbers:

a. $2 \div ? = 4$

b. $\frac{1}{3} \div ? = 2$

c. $? \div 1\frac{1}{3} = 1\frac{1}{2}$

Name:

Date:

1. Jodi gave her brother $\frac{2}{3}$ of the macaroni and cheese left in a pan. If the pan was $\frac{3}{4}$ full before she gave her brother his portion, how much of the pan of macaroni and cheese did he get? Show two different ways to solve this problem.

2. Brett is planting a vegetable garden. His dad said he could use $\frac{5}{8}$ of the garden plot if he promises to plant corn in $\frac{4}{5}$ of it. What portion of the garden will be corn? Justify your answer.

3. Make up your own multiplication word problem that uses the numbers $1\frac{2}{3}$, $\frac{5}{6}$, and 2.

Name: Date:

1. After school, the members of the math team meet at Dominic's for pizza. If you order one slice of pizza, Dominic gives you $\frac{1}{3}$ of the pizza. Most days Dominic cooks $6\frac{1}{2}$ pizzas for the math team. How many students does he plan to feed? Justify your answer.

2. You have $1\frac{3}{4}$ cups of chocolate bits. You plan to make chocolate chip cookies, and each batch needs $\frac{1}{2}$ cup of chocolate bits. How many batches will you be able to make? Justify your answer.

3. Make up a story problem for $4 \div \frac{2}{3}$. Solve the problem using diagrams and pictures.

Name: Date:

1. A group of boys is learning to tie knots. Each boy needs a piece of rope $\frac{5}{8}$ of a yard long. How many boys can cut a piece from a hank of rope 6 yards long?

2. A garden bed is $4\frac{1}{2}$ feet long. You want garden sections that are $\frac{3}{4}$ feet long. How many sections of the garden will you have?

3. Gail has $1\frac{3}{8}$ pounds of peanuts. Dave has $2\frac{3}{4}$ pounds of almonds. If they mix their nuts together, how many pounds of nuts will they have?

4. My birthday party was held at Dave's Pizza. There were only two tables in this small restaurant. One table sat 4 people and the other table sat 8 people. Mom bought 10 pizzas and put 3 pizzas on the table that sat 4 people and 7 pizzas on the table that sat 8 people. Which table had more pizza per person? Explain your thinking.

Name: Date:

1. At the beginning of the marathon, only two-fifths of the runners began to run when the gun fired. If 460 racers began to run, how many racers were there in all?

2. There were a number of candy bars in a jar. Kai took $\frac{1}{6}$ of them. Melia took $\frac{1}{4}$ of what was left. Now there are 15 candy bars. How many candy bars were there in the beginning?

3. Cindy answered $\frac{5}{6}$ of the questions on her math test correctly. She also knows she got 18 of the first 27 questions correct. How many questions were on her test?

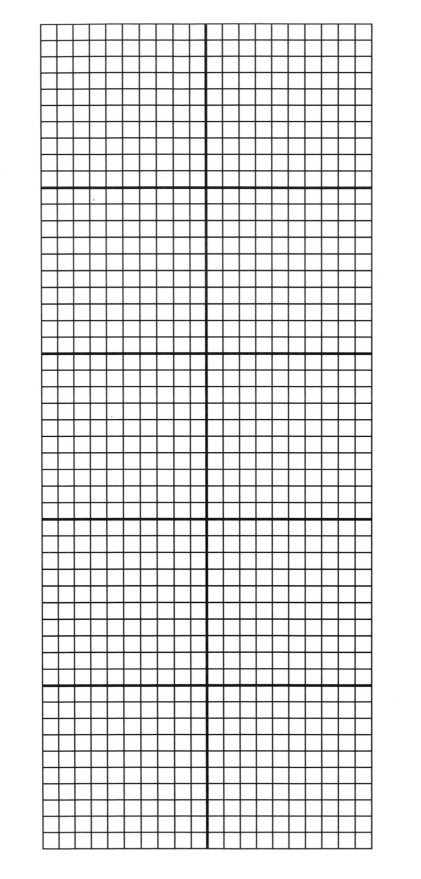

THOUSANDTHS GRID

WHAT'S MY NUMBER?

Name: Date:

Use the clues below to find the correct numbers.

1. The number is between 4 and 5.

   It takes four digits to name the number.

   The digit in the tenths place is one-fourth the digit in the hundredths place.

   The digit in the thousandths place is three times the digit in the tenths place.

   The digit in the tenths place is half the digit in the ones place.

   What number meets these clues?

2. The number is between 8 and 9.

   It takes four digits to name the number.

   The digit in the thousandths place is twice the digit in the tenths place.

   The digit in the hundredths place is three times the digit in the tenths place.

   The digit in the thousandths place is half the digit in the ones place.

   What number meets these clues?

3. Make up a list of clues to identify a number. Exchange your clues with a classmate and find the number that is described.

Zeroing in on Number and Operations: Key Ideas and Common Misconceptions, Grades 5–6 by Anne Collins and Linda Dacey. Copyright © 2010. Stenhouse Publishers.

Name: Date:

Use the grids below to show the decimal conversion for the given fractions.

$$\frac{3}{5}$$

$$\frac{5}{8}$$

$$\frac{4}{5}$$

$$\frac{3}{8}$$

$$\frac{5}{6}$$

$$\frac{2}{3}$$

Zeroing in on Number and Operations: Key Ideas and Common Misconceptions, Grades 5–6 by Anne Collins and Linda Dacey. Copyright © 2010. Stenhouse Publishers.

EQUIVALENT FRACTIONS AND DECIMALS CARDS

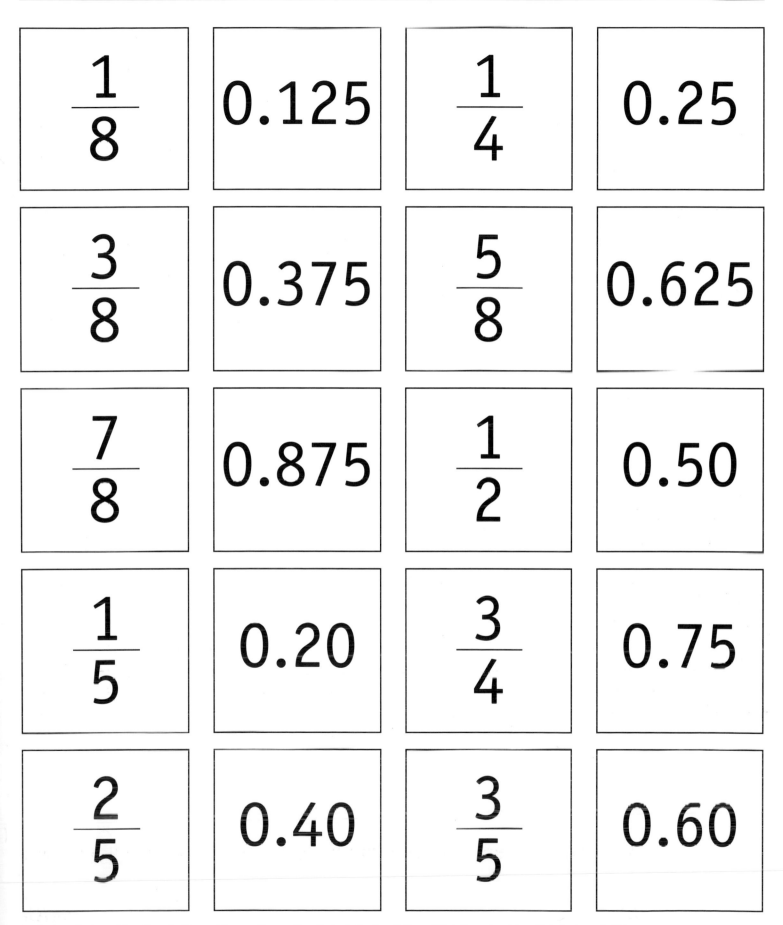

$\frac{1}{8}$	0.125	$\frac{1}{4}$	0.25
$\frac{3}{8}$	0.375	$\frac{5}{8}$	0.625
$\frac{7}{8}$	0.875	$\frac{1}{2}$	0.50
$\frac{1}{5}$	0.20	$\frac{3}{4}$	0.75
$\frac{2}{5}$	0.40	$\frac{3}{5}$	0.60

Name: Date:

1. Aiden wrote the following number sentence: 3.7 + 0.22 = 5.9. Use estimation to show Aiden he is mistaken.

2. Billy's time in the 440-yard race was recorded at 0.5 seconds. What is the range of possible times he could have finished?

3. This table shows the average monthly rainfall or snowfall amounts in Boston, Massachusetts. About how many total inches of rain, rounded to the nearest inch, will fall during June, July, and August? Be sure to give a range of inches!

Month	Inches	Month	Inches
Jan.	3.92	July	3.06
Feb.	3.30	Aug.	3.37
Mar.	3.85	Sept.	3.47
Apr.	3.60	Oct.	3.79
May	3.24	Nov.	3.98
June	3.22	Dec.	3.23

4. Because of severe weather in June 2009, rainstorms dropped 6.68". About how much more rain fell in June 2009 than the average expected rainfall of 3.22"?

5. How does an estimate help you determine the reasonableness of your answer?

Zeroing in on Number and Operations: Key Ideas and Common Misconceptions, Grades 5–6 by Anne Collins and Linda Dacey. Copyright © 2010. Stenhouse Publishers.

Name: Date:

1. Donovan bought two pencils, one eraser, one notebook, and one pen. How much change did he receive from a $20 bill?

School Supplies	Cost
Pen	$1.99
Pencil	$0.49
Paper	$2.39
Eraser	$0.75
Notebook	$3.39

2. Nick has a $5 bill. He wants to buy as many items as possible. What can he buy?

3. Jeri says that $4 - 3.754 = 3.75$. Explain to her why she is incorrect.

4. Same shapes have same values. Find the value of each shape.

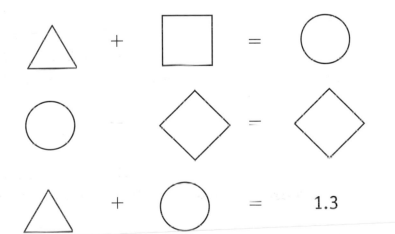

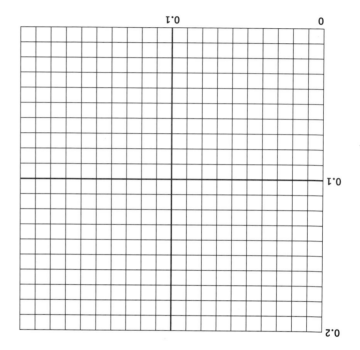

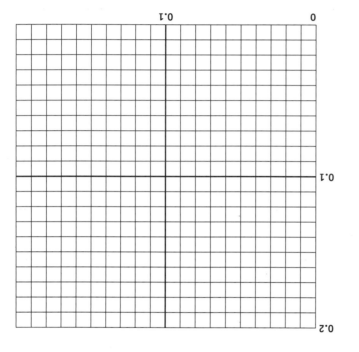

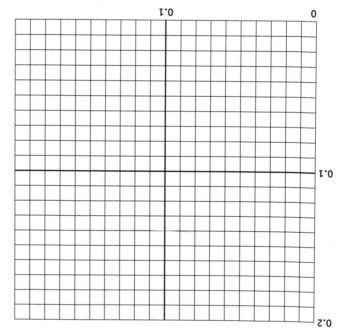

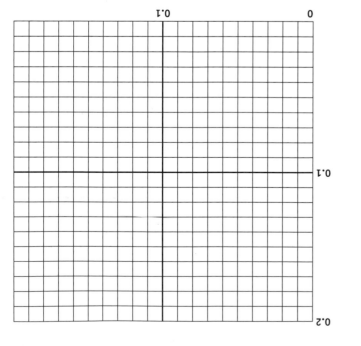

DECIMAL MULTIPLICATION GRIDS

DECIMAL MULTIPLICATION TABLES

Name: Date:

Factor (Tenths)	Factor (Tenths)	Product

Factor (Tenths)	Factor (Tenths)	Product

Factor (Tenths)	Factor (Tenths)	Product

Factor (Tenths)	Factor (Tenths)	Product

Zeroing in on Number and Operations: Key Ideas and Common Misconceptions, Grades 5–6 by Anne Collins and Linda Dacey. Copyright © 2010. Stenhouse Publishers.

Name: Date:

1. It took Mary 4.5 hours to travel the 282.5 miles to Sacramento. What was Mary's average speed?

2. Ken needs to fill a piñata for a party. The price of one candy bar is $0.65. How many candy bars can Ken buy with his $20.00 bill?

3. Kevin wants to know approximately how many baskets he can shoot in 6.5 minutes if it takes him 0.03 minutes per shot.

4. A painter had 25 L of paint. He used 2.5 L of paint every hour. He finished the job in 5.5 hours. How much paint did he have left?

The digits in the computation below are all correct, but the decimal point has been removed.

$$157 \div 8 = 19625$$

Use only estimation to find the quotients of the following. Write a rationale for each answer, then check your answers using a calculator. If you are incorrect, fix the answer and your rationale.

a. $157 \div 0.8$

b. $1.57 \div 8$

c. $15.7 \div 0.8$

d. $157 \div 80$

Name: Date:

1. Jeanne is saving her allowance money. She saves $2.25 each week. Complete the rate table to find out how much money she will save over different periods of time.

Weeks	2	4	6	8	12	24	36	52
Money								

2. Maria and Rosaria are participating in a fund-raising walk. Maria decided to ask her friends to sponsor her for $0.75 per mile. Rosaria decided to ask her friends to sponsor her for $2.00 plus $0.50 per mile.

   a. How much money will each girl raise if they each complete 3 miles? 5 miles? 8 miles? 15 miles?

   b. Which is the better plan if the goal is to raise the most money?

3. Manny is buying oranges for his soccer team. He needs to purchase 3 dozen oranges. He checks out the cost at Food Mart and finds they cost 3 for $1.29. He also prices the oranges at Food for Less and finds they cost $5.99 per dozen.

   a. Make a rate table to show the cost of 3 dozen oranges at Food Mart and Food for Less.

   b. Which is the better buy? Justify your answer.

   c. Show how you can solve this problem a different way.

ANSWER KEY

A1. Thinking About Millions and Billions

1. 1,000 millions
2. About 32 years
   60 seconds × 60 minutes × 24 hours is 86,400 seconds in one day. 365.25 days × 86,400 seconds is 31,557,600 seconds in one year. 1,000,000,000 ÷ 31,557,600 is equal to 31.68 years.
3. Multiple answers are possible. Some examples may include: a billion homework problems, a billion chores to complete.
4. Multiples answers are possible. If you counted to one billion it would take you about 95 years, if you were given $1 a day, seven days a week, it would take about 2,738 years to get to a billion dollars.

A2. Place-Value Game Cards

Multiple answers are possible, depending on how many cards students are playing with.

A5. What Is the Mystery Number?

2,587,346

A6. Math Wonder

If the student calculates accurately, the starting number will recur in each starburst.

A7. Sieve of Eratosthenes

1̸	②	③	4̸ 2	⑤	6̸ 2,3	⑦	8̸ 2	9̸ 3	1̸0̸ 2,5
11	1̸2̸ 2,3	13	1̸4̸ 2,7	1̸5̸ 3,5	1̸6̸ 2	17	1̸8̸ 2,3	19	2̸0̸ 2,5
2̸1̸ 3,7	2̸2̸ 2	23	2̸4̸ 2,3	2̸5̸ 5	2̸6̸ 2	2̸7̸ 3	2̸8̸ 2,7	29	3̸0̸ 2,3,5
31	3̸2̸ 2	3̸3̸ 3	3̸4̸ 2	3̸5̸ 5,7	3̸6̸ 2,3	37	3̸8̸ 2	3̸9̸ 3	4̸0̸ 2,5
41	4̸2̸ 2,3	43	4̸4̸ 2	4̸5̸ 3,5	46 2	47	4̸8̸ 2,3	4̸9̸ 7	5̸0̸ 2,5
5̸1̸ 3	5̸2̸ 2	53	5̸4̸ 2	5̸5̸ 5	5̸6̸ 2,7	5̸7̸ 3	5̸8̸ 2	59	6̸0̸ 2,3,5
61	6̸2̸ 2	6̸3̸ 3	6̸4̸ 2	6̸5̸ 5	6̸6̸ 2	67	6̸8̸ 2	6̸9̸ 3	7̸0̸ 2,5
71	7̸2̸ 2,3	73	7̸4̸ 2	7̸5̸ 3,5	7̸6̸ 2	7̸7̸ 7	7̸8̸ 2,3	79	8̸0̸ 2,5
8̸1̸ 3	8̸2̸ 2	83	8̸4̸ 2,3	8̸5̸ 5	8̸6̸ 2	8̸7̸ 3	8̸8̸ 2	89	9̸0̸ 2,3,5
9̸1̸ 7	9̸2̸ 2	9̸3̸ 3	9̸4̸ 2	9̸5̸ 5	9̸6̸ 2,3	97	9̸8̸ 2	9̸9̸ 3	1̸0̸0̸ 2,5

A8. Building Prime Factorization

1. five shapes: 2, 2, 3, 5, 5
2. four shapes: 3, 3, 7, 11
3. five shapes: 3, 3, 5, 7, 7
4. six shapes: 3, 3, 7, 7, 11, 11

A9. Multiplication Menus and Division

1. 15 cards
2. 23 weeks
3. 27 friends

A10. Show How It Works

No answer.

A11. Venn Diagram

No answer.

A12. For What Am I Looking?

1. November 30
2. 7 cm; 11 pieces
3. 4 feet by 4 feet
4. the 20th caller
5. 10 students

A13. Vocabulary Builder

No answer.

A14. Making Sense of Remainders

1. $4\frac{1}{4}$ cookies
2. $16.50
3. Multiple answers are possible but all groupings should total 187 students. For example, one suggestion would be to have 32 teams of six players and one team of five players, with one player on that team taking two turns.
4. 63 buses
5. 102 bags
6. $22.12
7. Multiple answers are possible.

A15. Estimation Bingo

No answer.

A16. Order of Operations Cards

No answer.

A17. Four Fours

The following are sample computations but others are possible.

$4 \times 4 \div 4 \div 4$	$= 1$	$4 \quad 4 \quad 4 \quad 4$	$= 11^*$	$4! - 4 + 4 \div 4$	$= 21$
$4 \div 4 + 4 \div 4$	$= 2$	$4 \times 4 - \sqrt{4} - \sqrt{4}$	$= 12$	$4 + 4 \times 4 + \sqrt{4}$	$= 22$
$4 + 4 + 4 \div 4$	$= 3$	$4! \div \sqrt{4} + 4 \div 4$	$= 13$	$4! - \sqrt{4} + 4 \div 4$	$= 23$
$4 - 4 + \sqrt{4} + \sqrt{4}$	$= 4$	$4 + 4 + 4 + \sqrt{4}$	$= 14$	$4 \times 4 + 4 + 4$	$= 24$
$4 \div 4 + \sqrt{4} + \sqrt{4}$	$= 5$	$4 \times 4 - 4 \div 4$	$= 15$	$4! + \sqrt{4} - 4 \div 4$	$= 25$
$4 - 4 + 4 + \sqrt{4}$	$= 6$	$4 + 4 + 4 + 4$	$= 16$	$4 \quad 4 \div \sqrt{4} + 4$	$= 26$
$4 + 4 - 4 \div 4$	$= 7$	$4 \times 4 + 4 \div 4$	$= 17$	$4! + 4 - 4 \div 4$	$= 27$
$\sqrt{4} + \sqrt{4} + \sqrt{4} + \sqrt{4}$	$= 8$	$4 \times 4 + 4 \div \sqrt{4}$	$= 18$	$4! + 4 + 4 - 4$	$= 28$
$4 + 4 + 4 \div 4$	$= 9$	$4! - 4 - 4 \div 4$	$= 19$	$4! + 4 + 4 \div 4$	$= 29$
$4 + 4 + 4 - \sqrt{4}$	$= 10$	$4! - 4 + 4 - 4$	$= 20$	$4 \times 4 \times \sqrt{4} - \sqrt{4}$	$= 30$

*11 can be calculated if decimals are used. For example, $4 \div 0.4 + 4 \div 4$.

A18. Fraction Cards
No answer.

A19. Comparing Fractions Cards
No answer.

A20. Pattern Blocks
No answer.

A21. Modeling Addition and Subtraction with Pattern Blocks
1. $\frac{1}{3} + \frac{1}{2} = \frac{5}{6}$

2. ⬡ − △ = ▱

$\frac{1}{2} - \frac{1}{6} = \frac{1}{3}$

3. ▱

4. $1 + \frac{1}{3} = \frac{4}{3}$ or $1\frac{1}{3}$

A22. Problems with Fractions
1. $1\frac{9}{12}$ or $1\frac{3}{4}$

2. No, he doesn't have enough because he needs 3 cups and he has only $2\frac{23}{24}$ cups.

3. $4\frac{1}{8}$ miles

A23. Model and Solve
Many models can be used. These solutions used pattern blocks so if your students use other models check for their accuracy.

a. Take $\frac{1}{3}$ and repeat it 8 times.

Answer: $2\frac{2}{3}$

b. Take $2\frac{1}{6}$ and repeat it 3 times

Answer: $6\frac{1}{2}$

c. Take $\frac{1}{3}$ and repeat it $2\frac{1}{2}$ times

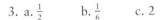

Answer: $\frac{5}{6}$

d. Take $1\frac{1}{2}$ and repeat it $3\frac{1}{3}$ times

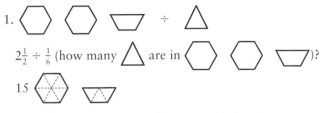

Answer: 5

A24. Understanding Division with Fractions

1.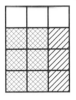

$2\frac{1}{2} \div \frac{1}{6}$ (how many ▲ are in ⬡ ⬡ ⬭)?

15 ⬡ ⬭

2. No, Chris is not correct. There are 8 halves in the hexagons and $\frac{2}{3}$ of the next half.

3. a. $\frac{1}{2}$ b. $\frac{1}{6}$ c. 2

A25. What's My Product?

1.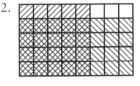

$\frac{2}{3} \times \frac{3}{4} = \frac{6}{12}$ or $\frac{1}{2}$

2.

$\frac{5}{8} \times \frac{4}{5} = \frac{4}{8}$ or $\frac{1}{2}$

3. Multiple answers are possible.

A26. Let's Share or Group!

1. Dominic plans to feed 19 people.
2. You'll be able to make $3\frac{1}{2}$ batches.
3. Multiple answers are possible.

A27. Area Division of Fractions

No answer.

A28. Posing Problems

Multiple answers are possible for each problem. Some examples are:
1. Mike ate one-fourth of three pizzas. How many pizzas did Mike eat?
2. How many fractions will there be in the sixth row? What will be the fraction in the middle of the tenth row? How would you describe the pattern in the first numbers of each row?
3. $\frac{1}{6}$: How much longer did Penny spend on her reading homework than her math homework?
4. $\frac{1}{3}$: How much longer than Penny did Louis spend on math homework?

A29. Problem Solving, Part One

1. 9 boys

2. 6 sections
3. $4\frac{1}{8}$ pounds
4. the table with 8 people sharing 7 pizzas

A30. Problem Solving, Part Two

1. 1,150 racers
2. 24 candy bars
3. 54 questions

A31. Thousandths Grid

No answer.

A32. What's My Number?

1. 4.286
2. 8.264
3. Answers will vary.

A33. Decimal Grids

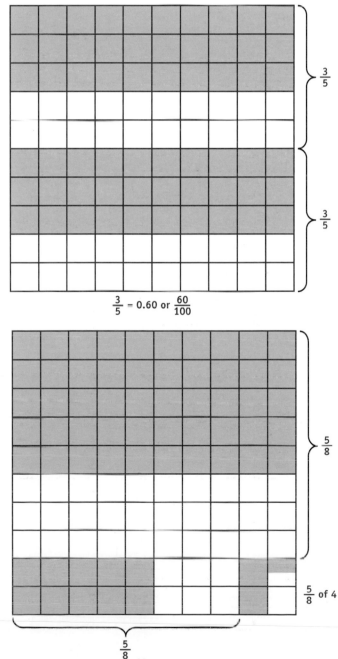

$\frac{3}{5}$ = 0.60 or $\frac{60}{100}$

$\frac{5}{8}$ = 0.62$\frac{1}{2}$ or $\frac{62.5}{100}$

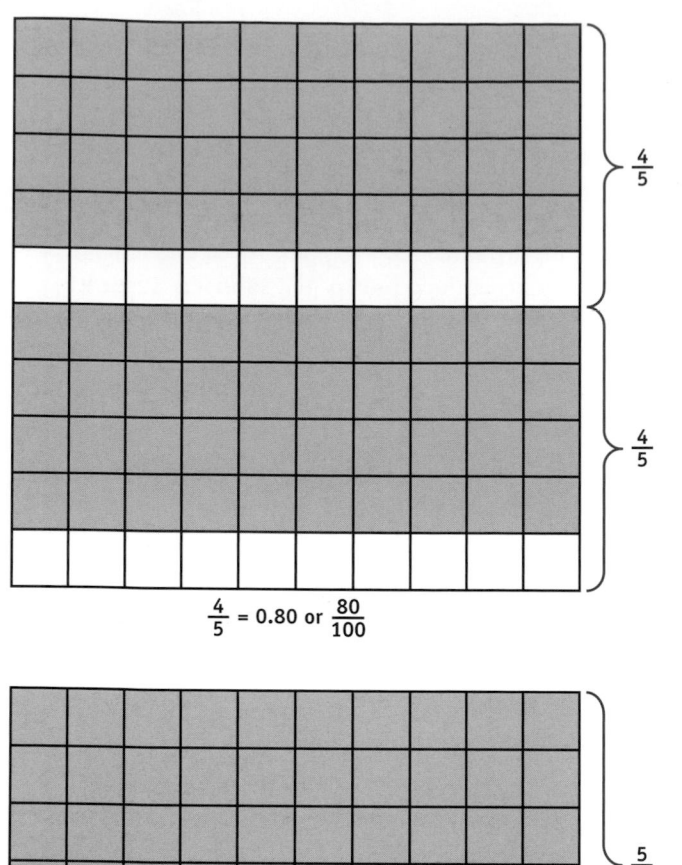

$$\frac{4}{5} = 0.80 \text{ or } \frac{80}{100}$$

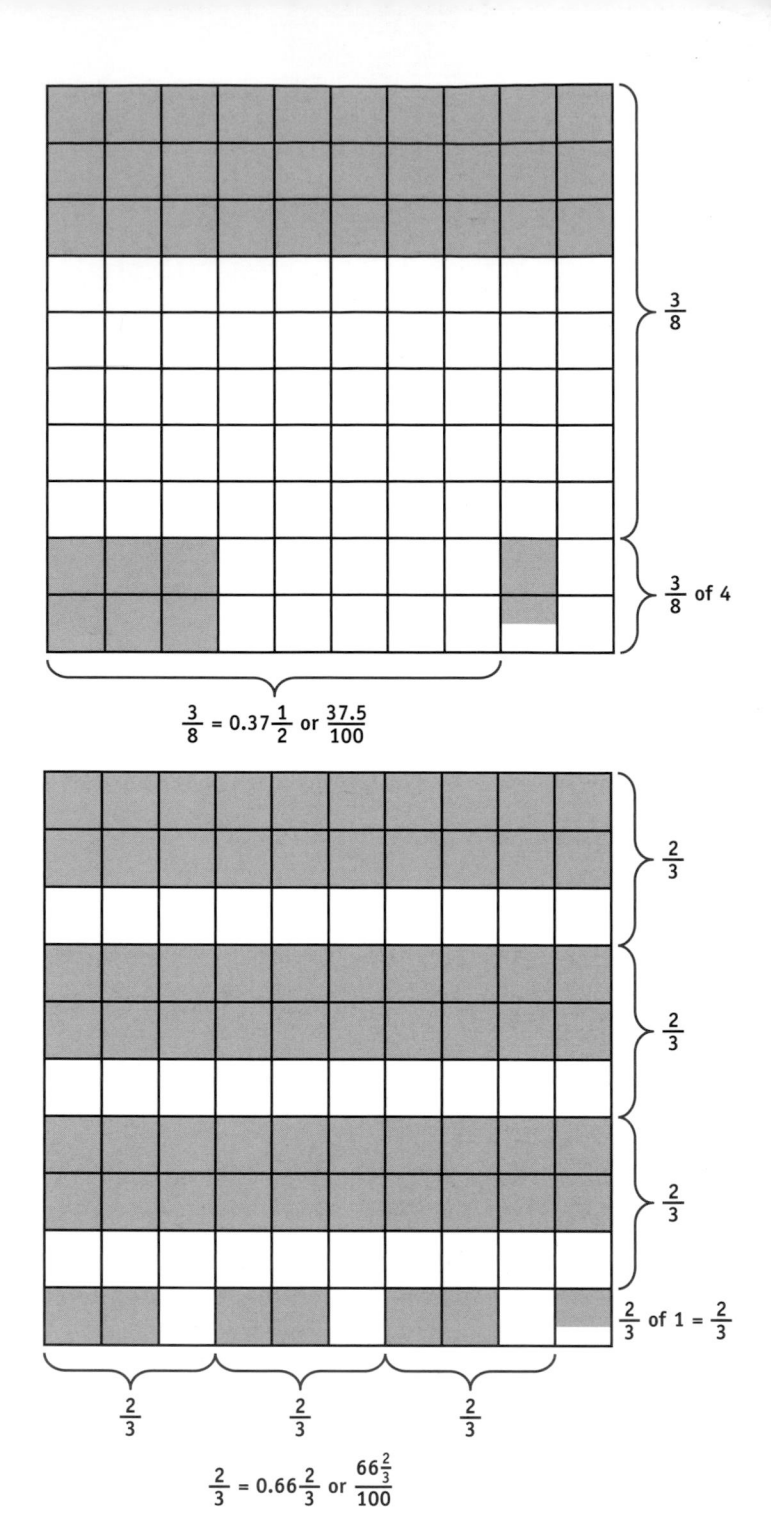

$$\frac{3}{8} = 0.37\frac{1}{2} \text{ or } \frac{37.5}{100}$$

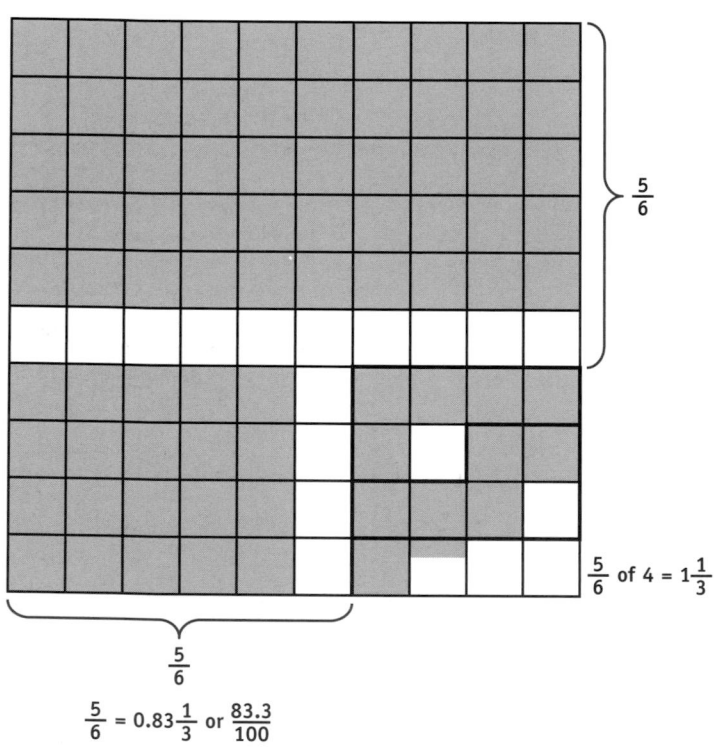

$$\frac{5}{6} \text{ of } 4 = 1\frac{1}{3}$$

$$\frac{5}{6} = 0.83\frac{1}{3} \text{ or } \frac{83.3}{100}$$

$$\frac{2}{3} \text{ of } 1 = \frac{2}{3}$$

$$\frac{2}{3} = 0.66\frac{2}{3} \text{ or } \frac{66\frac{2}{3}}{100}$$

A34. Equivalent Fractions and Decimals Cards

No answer.

A35. Decimals and Problem Solving

1. 3.7 is about 4 and $4 + 0.2 \approx 4.2$
2. from 0.45 to 0.54 seconds
3. between 9 and 10 inches
4. between 3 and 3.5 inches
5. Multiple answers are possible.

A36. Problem Solving

1. $12.89
2. Multiple answers are possible. For example, he could buy 3 pencils, 2 erasers, and 1 pen.

3. Multiple answers are possible. For example, $4 - 3 = 1$, and if you take away another 0.754, the difference will be less than 1.
4. Multiple answers are possible. For example:

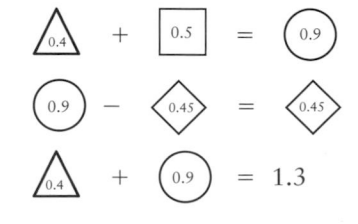

A37. Decimal Mutliplication Grids

No answer.

A38. Decimal Multiplication Tables

No answer.

A39. More Problems with Decimals

1. about 62.8 m/h
2. 30 candy bars
3. about 216 baskets
4. 11.25 L

A40. Where Does the Decimal Go?

a. $157 \div 0.8 = 196.25$
b. $1.57 \div 8 = 0.19625$
c. $15.7 \div 0.8 = 19.625$
d. $157 \div 80 = 1.9625$

A41. Solving Problems with Rates

1.

Weeks	2	4	6	8	12	24	36	52
Money	$4.50	$9.00	$13.50	$18.00	$27.00	$54.00	$81.00	$117.00

2. a.

Miles	1	2	3	4	5	6	7	8	9	10	11	12	13	14	15
Maria	$0.75	$1.50	$2.25	$3.00	$3.75	$4.50	$5.25	$6.00	$6.75	$7.50	$8.25	$9.00	$9.75	$10.50	$11.25
Rosaria	$2.50	$3.00	$3.50	$4.00	$4.50	$5.00	$5.50	$6.00	$6.50	$7.00	$7.50	$8.00	$8.50	$9.00	$9.50

b. It is better to use Rosaria's plan if you are going to walk 8 miles or less; it is better to use Maria's plan if you are going to walk more than 8 miles.

3. a.

Oranges	3	6	12	24	36
Food Mart	$1.29	$2.58	$5.16	$10.32	$15.48
Food for Less			$5.99	$11.98	$17.97

b. It is cheaper to buy 3 dozen oranges at Food Mart.
c. Multiple answers are possible. For example:

3 oranges = $1.29
3 oranges × 12 = 36 oranges
$1.29 × 12 = $15.48

12 oranges = $5.99
12 oranges × 3 = 36 oranges
$5.99 × 3 = $17.97

When teachers talk with students about their number sense and computational skills, they're bound to uncover some surprising gaps in their understanding. Knowing how to identify and bridge those gaps is essential for helping students at all levels advance as mathematical thinkers.

The *Zeroing in on Number and Operations* series, which aligns with the Common Core State Standards and the NCTM Standards and Focal Points, features easy-to-use tools for teaching key concepts in number and operations and for addressing common misconceptions. Sharing the insights they've gained through decades of mathematics teaching and research, Anne Collins and Linda Dacey help you focus on what students really need to know and understand at each grade level.

The 30 modules for Grades 5-6 are organized into three sections: Whole Numbers and Operations; Fractions; and Decimals. Each module begins with the identification of its **Mathematical Focus** and the **Potential Challenges and Misconceptions** associated with those ideas. **In the Classroom** then suggests instructional strategies and specific activities to implement with students. Each activity is supported by a reproducible (located in the appendix). **Meeting Individual Needs** offers ideas for adjusting the activities to reach a broader range of learners. **References/Further Reading** provides resources for enriching your knowledge of the topic and gathering more ideas.

At grades five and six, the authors focus on the key ideas that are essential for success at these levels:

+ Place value to billions and thousandths
+ Divisibility rules
+ Division with single and multidigit divisors
+ Order of operations to include parentheses
+ Multiples and factors to include least common multiple and greatest common factors
+ Rational numbers including equivalence between and among fractions and decimals
+ Fraction as ratio including the difference between an additive and multiplicative relation
+ Operations on rational numbers
+ Ratio and rates

Also available in the *Zeroing in on Number and Operations* series:

Grades 1-2 Focus: Counting, Number Sense, and Numeration; Meaning of Addition and Subtraction and Basic Facts; and Building Computational Fluency

Grades 3-4 Focus: Whole Numbers, Addition, and Subtraction; Multiplication and Division; and Fractions and Decimals

Grades 7-8 Focus: Number Theory and Integers; Fractions, Decimals, and Percents; and Ratio and Proportionality

Anne Collins is the director of the Mathematics Program at Lesley University. She has been providing mathematics content professional development institutes and courses for teachers for the past ten years and was recently elected to the NCTM Board of Directors.

Linda Dacey, professor of mathematics and education at Lesley University, works with preservice and inservice teachers, helping them to develop both their content knowledge and their practice. Her research focuses on problem solving, number sense, and strategies for differentiation.

Stenhouse
PUBLISHERS

www.stenhouse.com

ISBN 978 1 57110 798 5

90000

9 781571 107985

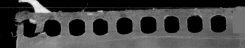

Grades 5-6

Zeroing in on
Number and
Operations

Key Ideas and Common Misconceptions

Anne Collins & Linda Dacey